Paul and Alta

Paul and Alta

Living Wisdom

Phyllis Pellman Good

Photography by Paul M. Schrock

HERALD PRESS
Scottdale, Pennsylvania
Kitchener, Ontario

1978

Library of Congress Cataloging in Publication Data

Good, Phyllis Pellman, 1948-
   Paul and Alta: living wisdom.

   1. Erb, Paul, 1894-   2. Erb, Alta Mae,
1891-   3. Mennonites—United States—Biography.
I. Title.
BX8143.E7G66   289.7′092′2 [B]   78-2890
ISBN 0-8361-1853-7

PAUL AND ALTA: LIVING WISDOM

Copyright © 1978 by Herald Press, Scottdale, Pa. 15683
Published simultaneously in Canada by Herald Press, Kitchener,
  Ont. N2G 4M5
Library of Congress Catalog Card Number: 78-2890
International Standard Book Number: 0-8361-1853-7
Printed in the United States of America
Design: Paul M. Schrock

10 9 8 7 6 5 4 3 2 1

To my parents
Richard and Betty,
for their living and
loving wisdom.

Contents

*We are still trying to find more
truly Christian solutions to
the problems we face.*
—Paul

A Prologue

A Prologue

I

Age sits easily on Paul and Alta Erb. It is climax for them—the brewing and seasoning resulting in a wonderful flavor. Here are two who have lived.

We Mennonites have been pilgrims in our impulses. "Moving on" has been our watchword. But how we live has always been bound up with how we believe. And Paul and Alta have lived. By watching their lives we know what they've believed.

First of all I witnessed their lives. Then I went to them to hear what they would say about the choices they made, about the reasons behind what they did. I was seldom surprised. For what they said was clearly borne out in how they lived.

This shall be a modest book. It was part of my agreement with Paul and Alta from the beginning. It was, in fact, the only way I could get them to go along with my little scheme. My idea—to preserve a natural resource, here in the form of stories.

As a Mennonite people we believe in the "wisdom literature" of the Psalms and Proverbs. This is some of our own. In keeping with our concerns for modesty and reluctance for publicity, let me suggest that what should be focused on here is what's been said, not who said it. But those of us who love Paul and Alta Erb can savor the personality and wit with which these lines were spoken. Having heard them say it gave me courage. I want to share their wisdom so more of us may have courage.

II

Here for the record and for fairness' sake are excerpts from two letters Paul wrote to me from Vermont: one before I started interviewing; the other after the project was underway.

"First of all we should thank you for the compliment you are paying us in the project you proposed. We are very human in the pleasure we take in being accepted

11

in allowing you to describe us in terms that we know we do not deserve. You should know us pretty well by this time, but we wonder whether you are not too flattering. People who know us better than you do, perhaps the people nearer our own age and who knew us in our younger years, may know more about our failures.

"You know that a good deal has been said and written about us. Where is the saturation point, beyond which people get disgusted and the writing becomes counter-productive? Of course, one doesn't like to be pilloried as a horrible example. But neither should one enjoy being paraded as a paragon of virtue, with the fear that readers will begin to think of things that can bring the idol crashing down. We are still getting some opportunities of service, and I guess we are afraid that these might stop if people begin to feel some resentment, even ridicule, against us because we consent to be set up as examples to be followed.

"This sounds like I am leading up to a firm negative to your proposed project. I do not mean that. I am simply telling you why we shrink from further exposure to either description or analysis. And we do want you to be fully aware of the hazards in what you are planning. Maybe you will not even be able to get a publisher.

"But we welcome you to come to Vermont and spend time with us in exploring your idea. You should feel free, of course, even if you come, to drop your idea as not a good one. We may even try to persuade you in that direction.

"If you can persuade us that there is a further testimony we can give, we should not be unwilling to do that. We are still trying to find more truly Christian so-

and approved. To put it more piously, we tried to live as God would ask us to, and can't help being happy if to some degree we have succeeded. This we hope can be a glory to God rather than to ourselves.

"But we are conscious of the danger of falling into pride and Pharisaic self-righteousness, even hypocrisy,

lutions to problems that we continue to face."

And later:

"Do you sense that maybe enough is enough, and if you go ahead and write your book, and it is published, there might be resentment somewhere? Please do not feel that for our sakes you need to press on with your project.

"We have had much winter since you were here. About four feet of snow on the level now, and we have had many mornings with sub-zero temperature.

"This week I gave a good deal of time to tying knots in comforters that Alta is finishing for the ladies here. Tonight we help eat a supper put on by the PTA."

III

Wanting to avoid the flattery they feared or a story unbalanced toward praise and away from their humanity, I asked Paul and Alta for a list of family, old friends, colleagues and students who would honestly answer four questions about them:

1. Describe Paul and Alta Erb's greatest strength or contribution, either as individuals or as a couple.
2. Describe a weakness of theirs, as individuals or as a couple.
3. Who is Alta Erb?
4. Who is Paul Erb?

The Erbs supplied me with names of twenty-one individuals, promising that if this group were honest, they would have not only good things to say!

My methods are admittedly unscientific. But then my thrust is not biographical research. I mean instead to capture the essence of two lives, with a little help from some who have known Paul and Alta longer than I have.

All twenty-one individuals responded to my questions. I have used excerpts from what they wrote in a

13

section at the close of the book. I hope these snatches give more dimension to my story. I hope, too, they will allay some of Paul and Alta's qualms about being adulated beyond recognition, or the truth.

IV

The straight facts about Paul and Alta Erb are many. Their benchmarks are varied and distinguished, at least in the Mennonite world. Here, as context, are a few essentials about the two characters whose words make up the bulk of this volume.

Paul Erb is a native Kansan, born near Newton on April 26, 1894, to Tillman and Lizzie Ann Erb. Alta Mae (Eby) Erb was born in Kinzers in Lancaster County, Pennsylvania, on February 23, 1891, the daughter of Abraham and Salome (Denlinger) Eby.

Both spent their childhoods in traditional Mennonite communities. But there was a common unorthodoxy about each home—education was valued and promoted. That force shaped these two lives, brought Paul and Alta within acquaintance distance, and had much to do with how they have spent their energies for sixty-five years.

Alta was a teacher first. She began at Hesston Academy in 1912 as a math instructor. Then tight budgets and miniscule staff pushed her into the area of teacher education. It is in that field that she eventually developed much of her expertise.

Paul's love was literature. He is famous for his passion for poetry and the literary greats. He, too, eventually joined the Hesston faculty.

Paul and Alta married in May 1917. They continued teaching, worked on master degrees and postgraduate studies, and with hardly a break in pace became the parents of Winifred and Delbert.

In 1940 the family moved to Goshen, Indiana, where Paul became a faculty member at Goshen College, and Alta too did some teaching.

Their next move was much more painful. After insistent urging from church leadership the Erbs set out four years later for Scottdale, Pennsylvania, the location of Mennonite Publishing House. The reason for the move? So Paul could become editor of *Gospel Herald,* the official weekly magazine of the Mennonite Church. The reason for the pain? Neither he nor Alta wanted to give up teaching. But church loyalty overcame their reluctance.

It was from this base that they began to be known churchwide. Alta's teaching abilities were put to good use as she worked as a Sunday school curriculum writer and turned out manuscripts on child nurture and children's literature. Her book, *Christian Nurture of Children,* (now out of print), sold more than 12,000 copies. It is the work of a woman full of love for children and wisdom for their parents.

For Paul, *Gospel Herald* editorials became his platform to speak to the larger church. He was no rookie to official churchdom; he had held offices regionally, pastored congregations in Kansas and Indiana, organized Mennonite Youth Fellowship (MYF), and served as Executive Secretary for Mennonite General Conference.

risonburg, Virginia, to teach when Paul was 75; to Vermont in an interim pastorate role when both were in their eighties. Paul's workshop on prophecy at the Mennonite Youth Convention in 1974 drew a larger crowd than any other seminar offered.

But enough background. Facts never add up to essence or personality. Here are Paul and Alta Erb, delivering their own words and ways, sharing their spirits as faithfully and energetically as they have lived.

But now he was read. And eventually he was at work on books on prophecy, doctrine, history, biography.

Speaking invitations flowed in for both Paul and Alta. ("Come alone or come together.") They have seldom said no. They went to Eastern Mennonite College in Har-

*This talk that a husband and wife must find out which
is the boss—that makes no sense to us.—Paul.*

1. A Love Story

1. A Love Story

It would be unthinkable to chronicle one of these lives without the other. It simply couldn't be done. Together, Paul and Alta Mae (Eby) Erb have found their ideals and wisdom and discovered how to live.

Paul and Alta enjoy each other. They still respect and amuse and disagree with each other after having shared life for sixty years!

It began with a good deal less magic between them. Or as Paul says now, "I wasn't interested in her particularly at first." Fortunately love sparked. It's held them together all these years.

The background to the love story is this. Tillman Erb of rural Hesston, Kansas, was business manager of Hesston College, and on the lookout for a math teacher. During a conversation with D. H. Bender, Tillman's second son, Paul, spoke up as "an inveterate reader of college annuals," and told them that Alta Mae Eby was a math major graduating from Goshen College. In the fall of 1912, Alta joined the Hesston faculty. Paul was a high school senior there.

Alta recalls her decision to come. "I would have gotten three to four times more money at the little schools around Goshen. But I liked the church. I wanted to work for the church. So I ironed for my board. Then I became dean of women." That developement eventually complicated the romance! Who ever heard of a student dating the dean?

Alta: "At Hesston I joined the Volunteer Band. We met at 5:00 a.m. Sunday mornings. Missionaries often talked to us. I had a leading for a number of years that I wanted to work for the church."

Paul: "I wasn't interested in her particularly at first. We were associated in the Volunteer Band. We both had a conviction for overseas mission work. Around the fall of 1913 she and I were sent together one day to survey for a Sunday school. That day I first became interested in her! Our friendship began in a common mission interest."

Alta: "But we enjoyed each other" (twinkle)!

Paul: "You insisted that the dean of women shouldn't have many dates. When I tried to get you just for myself, you said I would have to go!"

When the school year of 1913-1914 was over, Alta went home to Lancaster to spend the summer.

Paul: "Almost the whole summer passed without communication, but she sent me a picture postcard from Lancaster and said, 'Write.' Then I was spunky, so I didn't. But finally I sent her a picture postcard and said, 'Write again.' "

How did that sort of fencing finally lead to their marriage on May 27, 1917?

Paul: "I sensed here's a woman I can live with for fifty years and still learn something new from her. Our common interests were important. We both were conservative in our theology and devoted to the church. We were not afraid of intellectual frontiers. She had her own frontier in math, for instance. This intellectual reaching out—I knew we could grow together. We read to each other.

"I never believed any of this business about the inferiority of women."

Alta: "We never had a spirit of competitiveness between us. But then we were in different fields. When I started work in children's literature you helped me."

Paul: "We complemented one another. No, I don't feel we ever threatened each other."

Alta: "He knew something. It's still something I respect. He knew more than I did. Since he's getting older he forgets some things! I always felt the man ought to be a little smarter than the woman."

Paul: "We always kept in communication except for very brief times. I'm more expressive of emotion than she. Sometimes when we disagreed I was irritated. I'd try to go without kissing her and once she asked if I was

trying to punish her! So she saw me trying to be brave! We never turned our backs on one another. We had to apply our faith and the commitment of our religion to our relationship."

Alta: "We argued. I heard you say one time you like a woman with ideas you can argue with. But we never kept score. Married people need to compromise but you can't take turns compromising. You shouldn't keep those kinds of books in married life."

Paul: "We never threw rolling pins; we never got violent. She can be most exasperatingly quiet sometimes. A man explodes; a woman sulks. This is one of the differences between us. I like to discuss some things she doesn't even want to talk about."

Alta: "Well, if you admire a flower, you don't want to tear it all apart."

Paul: "You always liked to hear me preach. Always in my creative writing she was the first person I read to. She often gave me discerning criticism. So we were a pair in this way. When she had something to write she'd jot it down roughly and I'd refine it.

"I recommend a thorough partnership in marriage—everything I know she should know. One time in Scottdale I got a critical letter as editor of the *Gospel Herald* and I tried not to tell Alta. We sat down to eat and she asked if I got another nasty letter!

"Begin right. Make sure—as sure as you can—before you go into a marriage that it can succeed. Have basic agreements that you can both work from. Belong to the same church. Get together there so you don't always have to argue about that. You can avoid religious differences.

"Be slow enough about getting married. Expect to stay together. That gets people through some awfully rough places."

Alta: "Lots of people would stay together if they thought like that."

Paul: "I accepted marriage as a permanent relationship. It depends on the willingness of the two people to make it go."

Alta: "We never thought of such a thing as starting a divorce or separating."

Paul: "I recognize there are problems and I don't have a solution to every problem. So expect your marriage to succeed and don't go into it unless you think it will.

"An absolute essential to love is respect. As long as respect lasts, love lasts. Respect can be built into love."

Alta: "And grow in respect."

Paul: "Continue to become the kind of person your mate can admire. Share your lives. It's not just $1 + 1 = 2$. It's $1 + 1 = 1$. That's 1 with a halo around it. I'm sure there were times when one or the other of us just closed out the other with no tolerance. . . .

"We had one easy chair and I wanted another for many years. My wife didn't think we needed another chair, so we had to take turns sitting in the one. But then I brought it up again and we finally got a second one.

"She's more vigorous in her simple living than I am! It's a dangerous thing to send me to the grocery store because I always buy something that isn't on the list."

Alta: "I don't scold you too often, do I?"

Paul: "No. She manages the table, knowing the dietetics better than I."

Alta: "Well, you know there's something in the refrigerator I haven't opened yet!"

Paul: "You mean the celery!

"I don't believe in this 'his' and 'hers' business. I believe in 'ours.' If she had a pillow marked 'hers,' I'd be inclined to put my head on that pillow!"

A belly laugh from Paul. Alta nods knowingly.

Paul: "I'm first of all a churchman."

Alta: "Rather than a husband?!"

Paul: "Well, I haven't had much experience as a husband; I've had only one wife!

"But you've been a cooperative wife. You didn't mind if I had to be away often. Delbert said one time, 'Father just comes home and says hello and good-bye.'

"Alta's been first of all a teacher."

reading what I read. She's a woman of ideas on the broad scope. She is the mother of her children and has kept very close to them.

"She was a teacher and has never given up that attitude. She has a teacher mind. I think you can sense I'm proud of her. Some time after we retired from teaching she concentrated on preschool learning."

Alta: "Well, I want to keep up to date."

Paul: "Look at that! Age 83 and she wants to keep up to date. That goes back to why I got interested in this lady. I thought she'd be interesting to live with!"

Alta: "Well, I have a mind I'd like to write something—"

Alta: "Yes, I enjoy that most of all. I'm not a great housekeeper!"

Paul: "And she's not just Paul Erb's wife! She's always been a person on her own account. I know she loves me and appreciates me but she's in no way my slave. She has her own ideas and sometimes she doesn't agree with mine because she's always reading. She's not

Paul: "And she's changed her mind about things at this stage. You see it isn't true that old people can't change their ideas!"

Alta: "You have to when you see the evidence. Parents must arrange a child's environment so he can use all his powers. We don't have TV because I don't think very much of it. Mothers use it for baby-sitting, you know."

Paul: "Now if she keeps talking, you'll have to title this book 'Alta Mae Erb, with a few notes from her husband!' (hearty laugh)

"I'm proud of her!"

Alta: "If I had my children again I'd start them earlier with reading and arranging their environment—oh, Paul, I interrupted you!"

Paul: "That's the way she is!"

Alta: "Sometimes I think I get too introspective for my own joy."

Paul: "I'd call her a very spiritual person, and I respect that. Her friends know she prays a lot. Sometimes they share a need with her."

Alta: "People hesitate to give you requests for prayer. Until they're sure you'll keep them confidential."

Paul: "We don't share our spiritual lives too much. We don't lean on each other. We probably couldn't do things the same—it's a personality difference. Earlier in our married life we would have prayer aloud once a day together. Then we sort of dropped that. Especially if we had had an argument!"

These two have no use for a facade of ideal romanticism. Their love for each other is too deep for that. Because of that security they can own up to the differences between them.

Paul: "We had lots of arguments, lots of disagreements. But I'd hate to live with a woman who couldn't think up any ideas to argue back with!

"We ought to have our whole personalities married but it oughtn't to be static. You can have some things in tension. Any kind of growth means you're going from one place to another. If that's true in one personality, it's true with two personalities. You have to bring your backgrounds. That tension makes you arrive at some place different from where either one was to begin with."

24

But knowledge of each other's needs and weaknesses hasn't seemed to tarnish their mutual respect.

Alta: "He appreciates some people I don't appreciate—he can find something good in everyone. He has integrity. I don't doubt what he says." (Chuckle. . . .)

"He hasn't been willing to adapt to my hearing difficulty. And he doesn't like to be interrupted in his reading!"

Paul: "I'm impatient. I can say some pretty sharp things to you.

"I've always admired her abilities. And her faith, especially shown in her later years in her work of intercession . . . her religious integrity."

Alta: "Well, you grow in faith."

After sixty years together they still grant each other areas of privacy—not grudgingly, but with respect.

Paul: "If you get to look into that book [he points to the three-ring black-covered notebook lying on the kitchen table] . . . it's something I've never done. . . ."

Alta: "I don't think anymore of God being there and me being here and someone else in between. God is everywhere."

Paul: "I've learned not to interrupt her when I see her with that book."

Alta: "I started it in when I was at Hesston."

Paul: "There are maps in there, I understand. Then she prays geographically."

Alta: "Well, the overseas bookstores—I like to think where they are—it helps me see the church at work."

Paul: "She's not at all a clinging vine. It's hard for me to get her to take my arm! She's not a lover type of person. She doesn't shower affection on me. Oh, I know

she loves me! She's just not emotional. She enjoys literature but not in the same sense I do.

Alta: "I recognize him as knowing far more than I know. I think I act that way, don't I?"

Paul: "Um-huh. Sometimes when I say something you shake your head, no! But I guess it's good you don't just accept things without running over them for your own evaluation."

Alta: "I think the children ought to see the wife dependent in some things. Respect is an important quality for good relationships.

"Paul, you said many things I would say. I just think every person must be an individual.

"I think Paul's done a lot for the church. We've had a good life together."

Paul: "She tells me she likes to hear me preach."

Alta: "Oh yes, I could say that! . . . And he's very easy to cook for!"

Paul: "If you can make enough!"

Alta: "He's not critical of my housekeeping or my cooking.

"I wouldn't want to pick to pieces his personality. I don't think everything has to be blurted out. I think maybe we told too much about ourselves already. Did you think of anything I appreciate about you that I didn't say, Paul?"

Paul: "Well, we're different in a lot of ways and that's helped our relationship.

"Maybe that's one of the perils of modern life. Everybody looking at TV makes a deadly sameness!"

It seems destined never to happen to these two.

She was a mother and taught, too. She never neglected her children.—Paul.

2. Marriage and Careers

2. Marriage and Careers

Alta resists analysis in any form or shape.

So it was difficult to know if she was as innocent as she sounded when reflecting about what life is like when one is a mother with a full-time career. Paul forthrightly cleared up a few things, confessing to having done some legwork for her, helping her into a few roles she may not have sought on her own.

Those strokes of his are significant to the whole picture. Blessed with a wife of unusual abilities, Paul Erb has made it his business to help her use those gifts so that others might benefit. He knew she needed his favored position as a man to have the chances she deserved, so he went to work to create some for her. It was a sort of risk for him if she could not deliver. But neither of them can recall a time when she failed to live up to the opportunity she was given.

In the truest sense, they have cared for each other.

Alta: "There's too much being written about women's lib. . . ."

Paul: "I permitted her to be a person in her own right."

Alta: "And I never thought I was doing anything I shouldn't."

Paul: "More than once I underhandedly got her on a program when I knew she could do well. I created opportunities for her. When I became editor of *Gospel Herald* I got her to write a column on teaching Sunday school. I always respected her teaching ability.

"Knowing what the reaction might be, I suggested at first that she sign her column 'A.M.E.' And people thought it was my brother Allen! Then I got her to sign her full name and I got a letter from a brother who was concerned that through her column she was teaching men.

"I wrote back and said, no, the Bible says a woman should consult with her husband at home before she speaks and that's exactly what we do. She shows it to me; I edit it and print it!

"Just right here [Bridgewater Corners, Vermont] a man was teaching the Sunday school class and they needed a new teacher. They asked me. I know she's a better teacher than I am, so I suggested she do it."

Alta: "Oh, I don't think any of the men object...."

Paul: "No ... I was one of the movers in the reorganization of the church that said we need executive leadership from young people, women, and minorities."

Alta: "I don't think I ever gloried in the fact that I was doing men's work. I just did things because I was asked.

"I was asked to go to Vancouver and introduce the new Sunday school material, then come across Canada doing it. In Saskatchewan I spoke to 79 men in three sessions (in the afternoon one woman came in because she said she pitied me!) and they were so respectful.... I always worked for what I did. I used notes so it always gave me some purpose.

"Tell Phyllis about that family in Oklahoma."

Paul: "Why, this family is droll. Their church was quite conservative.... Their bishop thought no women should talk in church.

"When he died and the Sunday school was reorganized, a member of this family was named superintendent. He appointed a woman as the new primary teacher. The former bishop's wife stormed across to him after church and said, 'Don't you know women are to keep silent in church,' and he said, 'Well, why don't you!'"

Alta: "I think she was doing exactly what the Bible was speaking against."

Paul: "I've known of women's meetings when they'd invite a man in to have the opening prayer. In one conference they elected a man to run the business meeting of the women's organization!

"The WMSC [Women's Missionary and Service Commission] has had some frustrations in being just a sub-

sidiary movement because some leaders in the Mennonite Church didn't want the mission movement to be just for women. So the movement became just for men. I've spoken up for changes in these things.

"There's still one place though in which I guess I'm anti-feminist. I resist having a woman put on a committee just as a biological token. It's up to a woman to become qualified so she can bring something to the committee. The same with youth and minorities. Why do you want them just for the sake of having them?"

Alta: "In my day, the sewing circle was just for the older women. And there weren't activities for the younger women. . . . I don't think women aspired much to position."

Paul: "Certain dominant women kept silent at church but they said plenty to their husbands at home!"

One wonders if this tiny elderly woman does not really understand how unusual and revolutionary her behavior was. Her impluse to get on with things rather than discuss her own significance must have been as strong then as now. Or as she puts it, "I just never have had enough time."

Paul: "To show how her professional and family interests went together, Winifred was born in February of 1924 and Alta got her master's degree in August of 1924. I taught a course in reading for a couple of months while she had this baby."

Alta: "I was the only one teaching elementary education courses at Hesston and since we lived across campus I just invited the students to our house. I took Delbert along to geography class when he was three."

Paul: "She was a mother and taught, too. She never

neglected her children. Somehow, she could correlate these things and her children were better because of their mother's interests."

Alta walks carefully through this one. She looks for a balance for a woman with children—a mix between mothering and diversions from it. She thinks she would want to do more mothering, given another chance.

Alta: "To take a job where you have to go and stay all day—it isn't good for the mother. The temptation is for the mother to give her whole life to that job. I always worked ahead in the summers."

Paul: "I remember Delbert went to your geography class and he developed an interest in geography that will stay with him for the rest of his life."

Alta: "But I didn't do what I would do now. I'm an environmentalist. I wasn't aware then of all the curiosity God has given a child. You can arrange an environment for a child, take them to see things."

Paul: "If she were to do it again, she would spend more time supplying that environment."

Alta: "I think it might be awfully good for women to do a little something—meet people, get away from the irritation—have something just to be away a little and do something for somebody else. Do community things, sing in a choir."

Paul: "I was trying to think what her life would have been like without these other things. I think her life would've been constricted without them. But if something must suffer, the career probably should. When a woman marries she's making a commitment to being a wife and mother."

Alta: "Oh, and the children are so much happier."

There are sacrifices to be made, they believe. But not for a minute does either Erb assume that a woman, whether a mother or employed otherwise, is somehow less than a man.

Paul: "This talk that a husband and wife must find out which is the boss—that makes no sense to us. When you say the woman must be under the man, you mean not less than the man, just that somebody must go ahead."

Alta: "Even though I think I might know something, too!"

Paul: "Even though sometimes you think you know better!

"Some widows are shocked at their husband's debts. There's something wrong with a marriage if that happens. Now a man doesn't need to ask his wife if he may fill the car with gas. But the whole management of the estate must be a common thing."

Alta: "Well, we have a joint account."

Paul: "In some marriages the woman just sort of submerges and becomes his 'Mrs.' In others the man may yield.

"One thing that keeps me from being a male chauvinist is observing that God just didn't make women to be submerged. Many can't be happy unless they're growing.

" 'Becoming' is a strong word, a growing personality. That's one of the things that makes for happy old age—people who don't just sit and dream of the past but who are still becoming."

Alta: "It's a nice theory that you get lost in each other, but it just isn't practical, is it? Each individual just keeps developing."

Paul: "Somewhere you have to start bending toward each other."

Alta: "I guess you do because you go side by side, trying. But each one does keep developing."

Paul: "It's no sign for alarm. Even at our age you can say, 'I just don't see it that way.' Then you have something to discuss."

Alta: "Well, that couldn't happen in everything. You

must be together on some things. But you're still individuals."

Paul: "We are an 'I' and a 'Thou.' But the essence of marriage is that they become welded in a 'We.' "

Alta: "Well, you have those, *and* a 'we.' "

Paul: "Sometime, or again and again, married people ought to sit down and make an appraisal of their marriage. What's happening to us? What isn't happening to us? What are the hazards? What are the possibilities?"

Alta: "Well, it isn't good for all people. There's a danger in it. They get too self-conscious. You might damage something. Just like this place of woman. I never thought of it. I just did things. If you think about it too much you might spoil something. No two marriages are alike. . . . I guess that's part of Alta Erb!"

Paul: "Yeah! What she's saying now is typical of her. She doesn't like to discuss and analyze."

Alta: "Well, I just went on and lived. I don't think I ever thought of it that I was as good as a man. I thought about my work and tried to do it well. I wasn't showing off."

Paul: "We were studying 1 Peter here in our churches and we talked about woman being the weaker vessel. We decided if Peter were writing today, he likely wouldn't phrase it that way. But it's still true in a sense. If my wife gets a can of peaches off the shelf and can't open it, she calls me and I can. I think it's talking primarily about physical weakness. What does weakness mean?

"But we never had any difficulties on who was the boss. We never resolved that!"

Alta: "We just worked together."

34

You can adapt to any living situation (within limits) and be happy, if you're willing to make your children more important than your house.—Alta.

3. Children

3. Children

Both Paul and Alta knew they were special beings as children. Paul believes he learned responsibility and peacemaking at a tender age. Alta says she received her sense of self-worth from her grandparents and her mother. Her commitment to the church began to take root by witnessing Grandfather Denlinger's decisions.

Their own children arrived late with six years between the two. Paul and Alta believe if they were starting their family now, they would do many things the same—many things differently.

It seems that age has brought them new respect for youth. Now and then they wonder if they spent enough time and energy being parents. In fact, Alta in recent years has made the study of preschool children her specialty. She regularly sends new books on child development to her granddaughter Barbara, who is mothering three small sons in Morocco.

Alta: "When I was a child we had a sideboard that stood right down to the floor. Grandma emptied the whole bottom of that for me to play. Now I wonder why Grandmother gave all that space to me. I played with my paper dolls and furniture for hours on end.

"Grandfather had a furniture store and he gave us the old catalogs. We cut them up and furnished rooms for imaginary families."

Paul: "They had furniture without spending money!"

Alta: "He also gave us play space. Up in the loft we had a playhouse. We had five or six families and laid out their houses in this space. We gave them all money and had a store and gave them food according to the number of children they had! I think that kind of play in organization helped us—Brother and me, both. Grandfather told us we could keep it up there as long as we wanted.

"We did our chores first after school—bringing in the cobs and wood, sweeping the walks, trimming grass, whitewashing the fence—then we could play. We'd go to him as soon as we'd changed our clothes and ask him what to do and he'd be ready with our assignments.

"I thought I had a wonderful time as a child!"

Paul: "We had a large family. My father was away from home a great deal and we children all had our own work. I guess it was well organized.

"My father in his attitude toward property gave us the feeling that this wasn't everything. He didn't veer away from ownership of personal property. He gave us each a calf that we fed. When the calf was sold, he gave us a note for the money which he showed us. Then he'd borrow the money and pay us interest. It was in the context of family sharing.

"Our children learned to live very simply. I pity anyone who grows up in an abundant economy where they can get anything they want.

"By our children taking all the money in their banks and my adding to it we got a bike for $10. The children learned that buying is a cooperative thing.

"We gave our children allowances and they gave to the church out of that."

Alta: "They always budgeted. . . . And Delbert and his cousin were always giving chorus programs! Because his father traveled so much, you know."

Paul: "Our children's lives were richer because we traveled a lot and they went along. Since I was usually reimbursed for mileage, everyone could go along.

"There ought to be, in this day of the automobile, more family traveling projects."

Alta: "You know, I wouldn't be so afraid of criticism anymore in bringing up children. I'd let them learn to read. I wouldn't care if I heard that someone had said, 'I believe Mrs. Erb is teaching Delbert to read before he goes to school.'"

Paul: "Delbert built a railroad through six rooms of our house, and this made a mess of the house. Yet his mother let him do it."

Alta: "Well, with my second one I was more conscious

of God's possibilities in him. You can adapt to any living situation (within limits) and be happy, if you're willing to make your children more important than you house."

They did make a few mistakes, they believe.

Paul: "We had wanted to be missionaries and it didn't work out, so we hoped our children could be. Right before Delbert left as a missionary to Argentina we took a trip to churches, speaking about raising children, with Delbert and his wife, Ruth, along.

"He said to us one day, 'I should tell you folks something. When people used to ask me what I wanted to be when I grow up, you would always say, "He wants to be a missionary." It made me so mad I almost decided not to!' Well, God overruled that one! Too many parents try to plan their children's work, their marriage....

"We didn't use corporal punishment very much. I whipped Delbert twice and it was both in the same evening. He was misbehaving in church. A frown would usually break his heart."

The tables have turned. The children now care for their mother and father. But memories of the strategy it required to be parents burn brightly in these grandparents' eyes.

Alta: "I think children must know their father's vocation. A caring father keeps his children close. If he can't share his vocation with his children, he can't get close to them."

Paul: "The father can give time to his children, reading, playing, fishing. One time we were setting a date for a church committee meeting and Bishop John E. Lapp from eastern Pennsylvania was on the committee. We suggested a certain date and he said he couldn't make it because it was the first day of hunting season and he always went with his boys. We had to respect that—and I was glad."

Conclusion: Finding time for family was no easier forty years ago than now.

Alta: "You said, 'I think I have to go to a committee meeting,' one time, and Delbert said, 'I wish you'd get a new thinker!' "

Paul: "At times we decided there were things we

could do and things we couldn't and we just drew the line.

"Once when I was traveling through Hesston I called a man I needed to see. It was Tuesday evening and he said he couldn't. It was the evening he spent with his family. I admired that courage. . . . The home should just not always come out on the short end."

Alta: "You have to arrange for children's learning to take place. But you can't force it. They'll find what they need. It's not the amount of time you spend with them. It's the quality of the time.

"When we took Winifred home from the hospital the nurse said, 'Now you see that this child hears good music every day!' "

Paul: "It helped us get a piano."

Alta: "She was so good in church when they sang.

"Paul read to the children a lot. Do you remember how you read poetry to Winifred?"

Paul: "She loved poetry—those rhythms—even before she could understand what it meant."

These two aging parents indulge in delightful mem-ories, but not in glib platitudes, on the whole matter of children.

Paul: "Work with what you have. If you can't have family worship every evening, have it once a week."

Alta: "We were in a home where Sunday morning they all joined hands and prayed for the preacher and their teachers. And you should have heard the comments; they weren't formal either.

"You can build a lot of togetherness even if you aren't together. We saw one family take hands to pray before the children left for school. It started one morning when the one boy had a hard situation to face and asked them to pray. Then the mother did it too. So when the children came home from school, first thing they did was ask her how she got through it."

Paul: "One of our satisfactions in later years is our family. Their loyalty and activity in the church is a great joy for us. We don't take credit for it. We believe after all in personal decision. We gave them a rich environment, but that doesn't always work."

Alta: "Oh, they're not perfect."

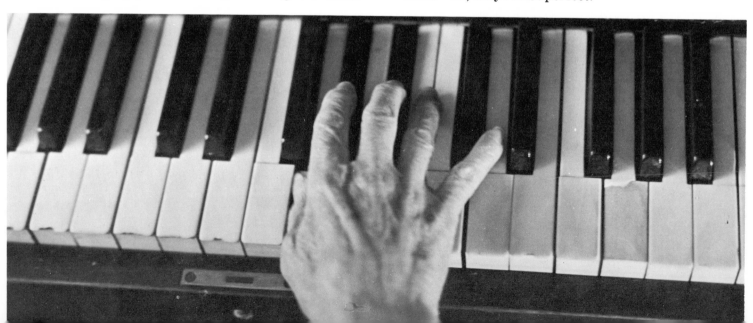

Now that young man we know who became a
millionaire—he has a problem.—Alta.

4. Possessions and Things

4. Possessions and Things

Paul and Alta believe in a mixture of planning and faith when it comes to the matter of money. They never worried about having enough money. If they worried, it was about having too much.

Now the complexity of this subject really hasn't passed them by. They raised their children during the Depression; they inherited neither money, a business, nor land; they have always worked for the church.

So what kept them from struggling to get—and then keep?

It seems there was design, and trust. Alta especially learned to make very basic decisions about what she and the family needed, or could get along without. Sometimes at the expense of celebration and joy, gently chides Paul!

"Limit yourself," they both agreed. "But," wondered Paul, "is there necessarily merit in doing without? It's a danger."

The longer the two talked, the less simple their understandings sounded. But one fact became clearer. From the beginning of their lives together they had made conscious decisions against possessing (and then protecting) things. They continue to make choices.

Paul: "Alta's father left home for twelve years when she was just a child, so making a little go a long way was a lifelong job for her."

Her lessons in economy paid off. And perhaps because of the example of her generous-spirited grandparents, with whom she and her mother and brothers lived, her thriftiness never became miserly. When the Depression hit, Alta was prepared.

Alta: "Day-old bread and skim milk was our supper for many months."

Paul: "And that was good food. We did well on it."

Alta: "Other people ate that way too."

Paul: "I can't remember we pitied ourselves."

Alta: "I canned spinach and that was pretty hard to eat. . . . If we had been the only family like that, our children would have squirmed more."

Paul: "We had a rich life though. Even in the Depression we weren't worried and we traveled. We knew the Lord would care for us.

"We offered to drop out of teaching because they couldn't pay us and pretty soon we got a letter from Alberta to come visit the church and lead evangelistic meetings and survey a community to get a mission started. Our Alberta friends had hams hanging in the basement for us."

Alta: "They gave us old coats and I made the children both winter and spring coats while we were there."

Paul: "I think our children knew we never worried. There was a sense of trust that things would always work out.

"One way we were able to get through those years was because Alta was a very good manager."

Alta: "When I went to Bethel to teach I had one good dress and one not so good. And I wondered if I'd need another dress. Today I get ashamed if I go to a church where I was two years ago and I have to take the same dresses. But I always have a new subject to talk about."

Paul: "It doesn't bother me at all to wear a white shirt, even though people say that nowadays only people on welfare wear white shirts. We wear our clothes out!

"It really cost me money to dress plain! One day when we were living in Virginia our grandson came to see us, hitchhiking in, or however he got there, with no baggage except what he had to sleep on—a sleeping bag. He had a pair of pants on with patches and some holes. Now my wife's a rugmaker. And people know that, so they give her rags and she had a whole pile of trousers there in the corner of our apartment. She thought Phil needed a pair of trousers so she told him he could look through the pile and pick a pair.

"Well, he nonchalantly looked through them but

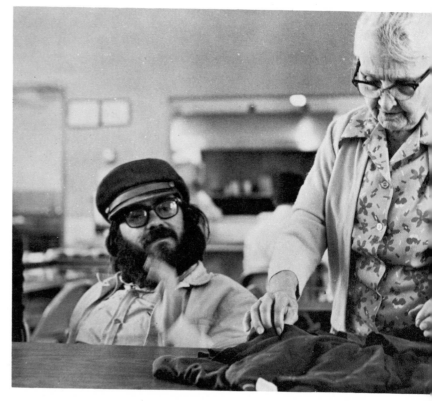

didn't take any. He said he already had a pair! Well, I had *many* suits!

"It's difficult to be totally simple. You can magnify the symbol of simplicity above the reality of it. Like the plain suit when we lived out West and had to send back East for a suit; then return it several times before it fit!

"We ought to preach simplicity but not legislate it. . . . Once I was in a church meeting discussing this and I said I'm ready to vote that all members of the Men-

44

nonite Church should drive a VW or nothing bigger, but then I don't have the trouble of long legs!"

These two have been blessed with good humor. What's more, they are keen observers. Watching others has taught them many lessons—and helps them draw some powerful conclusions.

Paul: "Evidently some people can control their income. There's a family we know that makes bricks. And at one point their business could have easily become bigger but they decided they didn't want it to and refused orders. . . . Business has a way of growing and pretty soon it's running you. I admire the courage of someone who can keep in charge. A man who gets into business and is successful is in an awful dangerous spot."

Alta: "I've often wondered how you can become a millionaire honestly."

Paul: "Don't let it appear I'm posing as an adviser to capitalists. I just know from reading the Bible a rich man is in a dangerous spot."

Alta: "And rich women too!"

Paul: "There's one thing these richer people can do— give free service. Get involved in projects like Menno Housing is one way—making good homes available for low-income people. Maybe it's acceptable to make all you can and give a lot away. There's no rule against giving more than one tenth. But there's the danger that others in a congregation think they don't need to give because you do!

"You can't draw lines for other people but you're lost if you don't for yourself. The church can help. . . . I believe in commitments to my brethren."

Alta: "Giving generously does away with a lot of

temptations, too. If you get things and get things, it just leads you on, doesn't it?"

Paul: "The early part of life is the time to lay up reserves. I'm not against that."

Alta pulled away from theory. She recalled fighting the battle, day to day.

45

Alta: "We never had a great abundance of sweets and rich foods. I could love it, cakes and things, but I just don't think we should."

Paul: "We've always done a lot of entertaining. As teachers at Hesston we made it a practice to invite each of the students into our home for a meal sometime during the year."

Alta: "And all our church members."

Paul: "But to do all this, we had to eat simply. Soup, or whatever. We have a conscience against seven sweets and seven sours."

Alta: "And the students loved it. We often had chili soup."

Paul: "I remember when the big home freezer first came out, I preached against it. I didn't see how any Christian could have such a luxury. Now if a freezer represents economy in buying, that's one thing. But if it simply means having all the food you want whenever, and overdoing it—that's a hazard."

In 1945 the Erbs left Goshen, Indiana, and teaching, to move to Scottdale, Pennsylvania, where Paul was to edit the *Gospel Herald.* Their children were young adults. Paul and Alta were responsible for the care— physical and financial—of the Eby's, Alta's parents.

Paul: "We sold our house in Goshen and went to Scottdale, intending to buy a house. People suggested we move into apartments there—one for us and one for Grandpa Eby's—while we looked for a house.

"But we soon saw that if we bought a house we'd be in debt the rest of our lives. I was fifty years old then. We liked to give and this debt would have hung over our heads all the time.

"And we discovered we liked apartment living. It suited us. We could live as we wanted and have enough left to give. It would have been wrong for us at that point to own real estate. If we had had small children, we'd have needed a house."

Alta: "But it was in another building and up five flights of stairs to get to my parents. And mother was an invalid then."

The Erbs speak freely, clearly at peace about their use of money.

Paul: "That's one thing in our attitude about finances—we're not secretive. I wouldn't hesitate to tell you that with our Social Security and Publishing House pension we get over $500 a month. I have a few investments which bear interest—some with Mennonite Mutual Aid, the Mission Board, the Publishing House.

"I have a conviction about that. I want all my resources to be working for the Lord; my talents, my money. I'm not judging anyone else. I'm not against the capitalistic system. I'm conscious again and again that I'm using it. I haven't renounced capital."

The Erbs are selective givers, supporting only what they believe in and know best.

Alta: "The radio has roped people into a lot of things."

Paul: "Our mutual funds with the church don't go into arms and whiskey. The administrators have a rule of thumb that not more than one tenth of any business in which they invest can be military. Sometimes it's almost impossible to locate a business that doesn't have any connection with arms or whiskey or sports.

"I'm speaking from the standpoint of the small investor. If I fell heir to $100,000 I'd have a different problem,

but I'm very comfortable about not having that problem!"

Alta: "Now that young man we know who became a millionaire—he has a problem.

"I feel the church needs to help us."

We were seated in the parsonage of the Mennonite Church in tiny Bridgewater Corners, Vermont. These two eighty-plus-year-olds had dared the New England winter by taking a six-month pastoral assignment here from November to May. Paul pointed to the upholstered

living room furniture, some of it worn to the wood from many years of use.

Paul: "One thing I felt good about is that the people here thought we could be happy with that chair.

"Now is there merit in doing without? This can be a danger too."

Alta: "I don't believe we lived simply to earn any merit from God. I believe I was open enough to Him that He would have convicted me."

Paul: "I think children won't be very happy if their parents maintain a standard of living much lower than the rest of the community. So there's a problem. You almost have to adjust to the standard around you or they won't want to bring their friends home. . . .

"When it comes to spending money Alta often says, 'This costs too much for the enjoyment we'll get out of it!' "

Alta: "Paul would like to ride the gondola over here to the top of Mount Killington, but I rode one in West Virginia, so I don't think I have to ride this one!"

Paul: "I'd still like to!"

Alta: "People's kitchens, you know . . . and the time people spend on expensive salads . . . I just feel I don't have the time for that. One lady had eighteen big cupboards in her kitchen—I counted them—and she knew where everything was!

"There's no one way of living. We have had fellowship with people whose way of living we didn't have to copy. You live your way without criticizing other people in front of your children. If you live simply and your children are happy, children catch on that they can have joy with little."

Paul: "We shouldn't be too critical of other people but we need to take ourselves in charge. . . .

"The Mennonite Church used to say we should live simply with capes and plain coats, but they didn't say how many we should have or how much they should cost. So this shows how difficult a problem it is.

"This tension is a healthy tension: how can we live a full life and still not be spending more money than we should? For many years we've given more than one fifth of our income."

Alta: "Now we have an advantage in our giving. We've worked at three church colleges and feel strongly loyal to all three. We want to help each of them financially."

Paul: "We're oftentimes giving to old loyalties.

"We are living with mobility. When they phoned and asked us to come to Vermont we didn't have to say we have all this stuff to look after. But then our business is with our minds and we can take them with us. It's different than if you have a farm and livestock. . . .

"We often cleaned house. When we moved to Winifred's we were cleaning house and Alta prayed one lunch, 'Lord, teach us what we can do without!'

"I take a certain amount of delight in walking through a big drugstore and thanking the Lord for all those things I don't need.

"I preach a sermon called 'The Pilgrim Mind,' remembering that we're only passing through.

"Why should you clutter up your later life with real estate?"

But these two aren't ascetics. With little effort they named a few things they'd like not to be deprived of!

Paul: "My wife thinks I read too much news!"

Alta: "I'd hate to give up my sewing machine."

Paul: "Maybe the Lord will have you braiding rugs in heaven! Maybe when I go to heaven I'll ask if they take *Time* or *Newsweek* there!"

Alta: "I'd hate to go to an outdoor toilet!"

Paul: "I couldn't live here without books, but I won't need to take them with me.

"It's very difficult to be totally simple."

I want to be where the brave minority is.—Paul.

5. Being Separate

5. Being Separate

Convictions grow; they don't just happen, the wise tell us. Here is proof alive. For Paul and Alta the stage was set early; the seeds were planted. It was the work of farsighted, committed parents and grandparents.

As children these two found their roots in the church. And when they were exposed enough to make comparisons with the rest of the world, they chose the discipline and security the church community offered for their lives.

Being separate had meaning, they had learned. It was valid enough to stake one's life on, they believed. The conviction has enveloped them almost all eighty years each has lived.

Alta: "Well, my grandfather read his Bible every day and he was so strong for the church. And my mother was a Sunday school teacher. One of the women said to me one morning, 'Your mother's such a good teacher.' "

Paul: "We both lived in church-centered communities. Our whole week was built around going to church. My father was a pioneer bishop in the West. He'd go to meetings in the East and come back with stories and this was high news for me.

"And the church school influence for both of us—when I was just forming my life's philosophy as a student, I was sitting under such men as J. B. Smith and J. D. Charles."

Alta: "By singing through the hymnal I got my theology. I sang through it many times out in the hammock. One time I'd sing every third song and the next every fifth!

"I went to public high school in Lancaster—the only Mennonite girl there—and pretty soon I started to go to the Vine Street Mission. And they began to ask me to do things. Pretty soon they asked me to teach. I gave some talks. And that just blossomed me a lot. Often I went to church three times on Sunday."

It was in the church community that they witnessed their best examples for living.

Paul: "One thing when we were getting a fixed life direction was World War I, when the Mennonites were a persecuted people. We identified with a minority and I've never felt I want to be where most people are. I want to be where the brave minority is."

Alta: "I'm sure the Volunteer Band at Goshen and

Hesston colleges helped me. I taught a class at Hesston called *Gospel Herald* where we discussed the church news."

Paul: "The heroes of my youth were the church leaders."

Alta: "We had to wear coverings with long strings but I don't remember it was hard. The public high school in Lancaster had a literary society and I was secretary of that. I was treated well. The teacher respected me. The other girls were nice."

Paul: "I don't think I was ever ashamed. You see I wore my plain suit at Bethel College and all through graduate school and I got used to being gawked at and known as the guy in the funny coat. Maybe that was hard on me. But I've found that it's good to be a Mennonite. I've found an increasing satisfaction in identifying myself. Mennonites are respected."

Alta: "Grandfather reading his Bible was my best impetus toward reading my Bible and praying, but I waited till high school to start. In college I'd get up at 5:00 a.m. and begin reading."

Paul: "We never went through a rebellion against a legalistic set of rules.

"Before I joined the church, the street carnival came to Newton and I wasn't permitted to go. I said when I grow up I want to be a Methodist, so my children can go to carnivals!

"But we didn't have a strict bunch of rules to buck."

Alta: "We didn't have a lot of teaching of laws, but one time a man came and preached against tobacco. My grandfather always smoked a cigar every afternoon. But that day Grandfather brought his box of cigars to the table and said he had a lot left but he was going to throw them away."

Paul: "After hearing one sermon! If he had fought it, look how that would have affected her.

"I don't like to be critical of the church."

Alta: "I can truly say I never did turn against the church. I saw some of the kindest people in the church. They lived. They were good neighbors. They weren't perfect. But they were kind, good people. They were respected and not seen just as some old narrow folks. They had a lot of mission work and it's still going on.

"There was one woman who wore a hat. She wasn't a Mennonite, but she taught the women's Sunday school class in a Mennonite church year after year."

Paul: "One thing that's kept me in the church is its biblical practice. I've liked its active program. I'm an activist and the Mennonite Church I've always known gave me something to do—causes to give to, a forum, a pulpit, something to bring my children up for.

"I've seen our church tried in the court of everyday affairs and opinion. A lot of people have good opinions of us. I'm glad to belong to a church in a minority position that receives that kind of respect.

"I don't take the position that no other people can be Christians, but there's no other church I'd rather be part of."

Alta: "Women taught Sunday school and at prayer meeting we could lead in prayer, and maybe that satisfied us."

Paul was on the verge of sounding like a patriot. It was insight into the depth of his dedication.

Paul: "The telephone company puts a phone in your house and you don't say, 'Thanks a lot. Sometime when I have the money I'll make a donation to the phone company.'

"When I drive on the turnpike and accept that little card, I don't develop my convictions as I go along. If the road's rough, I can't decide not to pay.

"We make commitments. So why shouldn't I make commitments to my church?"

Alta: "The church has given us a good living. They were very good to us here in Vermont. I don't keep track of it; I don't want to know if people don't bring me things."

Paul: "I've found the church a good employer."

Alta: "The church fathered us and mothered us! People were always interested in our children and work.

It's very supportive. . . . You get things on the other side though, but it was never enough to unbalance us. It didn't discourage me very much."

Paul: "Orie Miller told me one needs to have a very good reason to say no to the church. This has been my attitude too."

These two are not young innocents, fresh converts, untried troops. Their conversation rolled easily but never naively.

Paul: "One of the hardest things the church ever asked me to do was quit teaching and go to Scottdale. I thought I was a teacher. I was trained as a teacher. I did all my resident work for a PhD; I just didn't do the thesis.

"I stalled for a year and a half about moving to Scottdale. Harold Bender finally said he thinks I ought to go."

Alta: "It just kind of crushed you that you couldn't teach."

Paul: "I'm glad I did go. It added a new dimension to my life. And it didn't stop my teaching opportunity."

Some things the church asked were downright funny. But because loyalty was usually the issue Paul and Alta were faithful.

We were at the kitchen table, rifling through some old family pictures.

Paul: "Bird watching has been one of my hobbies."

Alta: "That's some hat you have on!"

Paul: "That's the kind we wore then! You know, they always said if God had meant for us to have a crease in our hats he'd have made a crease in our heads. I never had the courage to ask them about the brim!"

They have found almost total fulfillment in the

54

church. They permitted it to consume their energies, their best ideas.

People who choose other loyalties are shortchanged the whole way around, they believe. Other lures—and the people who choose them—make the Erbs angry. Righteously angry.

Alta: "This is the most sports crazy world! You can spend so much money just to sit and look. I saw enough games at college to know how much you have to take away with you.

"The world is just full of attractions like that to pull us away from things that are worthwhile. But sports don't quench your thirst, if you have any thirst for righteousness."

Paul: "I've been watching some of the Olympics, mostly out of curiosity. I enjoy the bobsledding.

"But she can just hardly tolerate this—me watching the Olympics for an hour a day!"

Alta: "Several hours a day."

Paul: "But she'll solve crossword puzzles, jigsaw puzzles, and I don't have time for that! So it just reinforces again, you can't judge or decide for other people. All Christians have to ask, should I spend my time, my money, this way."

Some distinctions are fuzzy when it comes to the matter of being separate.

Paul: "My father was a councilman at Harper, Kansas, and mayor of Hesston, Kansas. But I don't think he ever voted! That was quite an issue when I first entered the church, so I've never voted.

"I'm so disillusioned about a good man in politics. There's so much that's rotten I'm pretty well scared away from it. I'm pretty skeptical about whether one can really maintain his Christian convictions in politics.

"Oh, I keep up on politics! I'm an observer. But I can't insist on this for others. I don't answer all those questions about how we can benefit from government without participating in it."

But of one thing Paul is certain. His church has a peculiar mission to the world.

Paul: "Yes, more than ever. Just take those Canadian Mennonites who are storing tons of wheat until it's needed."

Alta: "Oh, what MCC [Mennonite Central Committee] is doing is just wonderful."

Paul: "Our Anabaptist philosophy is there.

"A small group like ours can have a kind of cohesiveness that makes a well-run program possible. We know our personnel.

"Our attitude toward war is more significant than ever. People are beginning to see just how futile war is.

"We stand out less now simply as a social anachronism. Our testimony in the world is both spiritually and socially more significant than it ever was before. People when they hear about our VS [Voluntary Service] program say, where do you get young people like that?

"Mennonites have a greatly increasing range of abilities to offer—and an increasing moral background. We do these things because we are spiritually motivated. We think that we ought to do them."

Alta: "The world knows that we stand ready to meet their needs. In a *Voice* [a magazine published by the Women's Missionary and Service Commission] they said they need 1,800 pieces of bedding for seven countries.

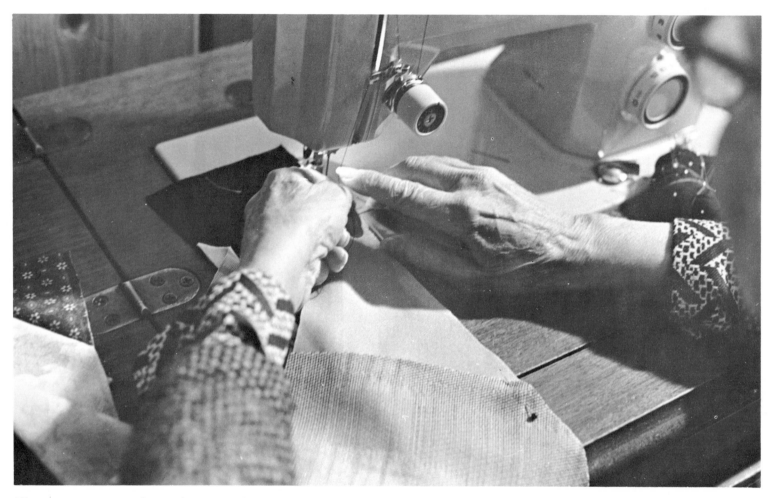

The requests came from the countries, so they know we stand ready to help. Health kits and sewing kits—they don't want our clothing—they want to make their own because they don't dress like we do.

"We've learned to sew. We've learned to give. And I'm just doing some of my learning now!"

They sound like campaigners. Paul and Alta are evangelists in the truest sense.

You can't draw lines for other people, but you're
lost if you don't for yourself.—Paul.

6. Drawing Lines

6. Drawing Lines

All their lives Paul and Alta Erb have said yes to some things; no to others. Now and then they've changed their minds about matters of principle.

Any line one draws can look ridiculous, they agree. Why draw it here, instead of here, is always a legitimate question. It's tricky business, to be sure. But that's never cause enough to avoid deciding for or against. As Paul says, "You can't draw lines for other people, but you're lost if you don't for yourself."

Paul: "The refrigerator we had was a Westinghouse we bought thirty years ago. It was good and it functioned well, but it had just a little freezing unit up in the corner. So my wife thought maybe we could get a little better one—"

Alta: "—one with a freezing unit the whole way across the top."

Paul: "So we went down to the appliance store and I took my checkbook to buy one—we could have bought one—but we went home to think about it and Alta said, 'With all the needs in the world, I don't think we should buy it.'

"Most of my life I drove Fords because they used to be more economical. So I've always driven economy cars because I didn't want to put money into mere styling. I wouldn't have felt comfortable in a big car."

Alta: "You'd have thought it looked inconsistent."

Paul: "Once I was riding with a man who had a big car, an Olds or something, and he had heard of some of my ideas. So he began explaining that he and his wife didn't like the vibrations of a cheaper car. We went back to his house and he had a big easy chair there. He told me to sit in it and pretty soon it started vibrating all over the place! He was explaining how healthy this vibrating was!

"Well, I get my vibrating in my car!"

Alta recalled a trip they once took when Winifred was a young girl, beginning to notice fine and beautiful things. The Erbs were hosted by a conservative Mennonite couple.

Alta: "At the supper table they set green glass dishes. In the morning they had pink ones—delicate pink, it was. And Winifred said, 'Mother, you saw the beautiful ones in the china closet, and then I saw another set in the kitchen,' so they had four sets! I told her, 'They like dishes like we like books!'

"It was good for Winifred to see it herself rather than for me to say it. We ought to get the attitude and the idea first, and then get the word.

"On that same trip she saw a lady step out of a car in a very straight, plain dress with points and gores. But she spied her gorgeous purple petticoat with lace—it was 'fussy' as Winifred called it!

"I'd say I'm nonconformed in setting a table. I wouldn't have felt right to take the time or the money to serve a fancy meal on expensive dishes. It wouldn't be good for my soul to prepare a meal for people to talk about. Oh, it's an art, but it shouldn't consume too much time or money or show, nor be done for one person and not for someone else. It's a hard line to draw. Time was always the problem for me. It still is."

Paul: "I think maybe the young people today have accepted the real principles of nonconformity."

Alta: "We had more legalism."

Paul: "I think the young people are reexpressing it—having their struggles, of course, but not conforming to high society styles. Of course, the motives may not always be religious."

Alta: "If a new style of furniture came out, people would get the latest. Same as today; keep up on the kitchens!"

Paul: "Some Mennonites drove Packards and Cadillacs."

Alta: "I guess they could afford them!"

Paul: "Of course, but they were always black!"

Alta: "I don't think if you live simply you're necessarily Christian, but if you are a Christian I think you'll live simply."

Paul: "Expensive vacations and trips—"

Alta: "All sports are very expensive—"

Paul: "But we are affluent and it doesn't occur to enough of us to challenge those shibboleths."

Alta: "We were at a house once and the Mother said, 'See if there's room to hang your things in that closet. Just push those dresses back. I hardly wear them except for special occasions.'"

Paul: "Mennonites are taking all kind of trips these days, tours to the Holy Lands and other interesting countries. That's a better way to spend our money than eating it, I guess. But we must always keep making judgments about these things. We can't insist on our solution being taken by others."

Alta: "We were taken out to eat once and it cost $15.00 a plate. And we both got sick! It was too rich!"

Paul: "I've been much freer to buy books than to spend our money on eating out. For years I had kind of a rule—a book a week."

Alta: "Oh, Paul, you never did that!"

Paul: "Yes, I did when I was accumulating a library. But I mustn't judge others if they don't come to the conclusions I do.

"I guess there is a certain elitism in it. I have a certain pride in my acquaintance with literature."

How does a man with such a no-nonsense view of things justify his love for poetry and all his years of living, breathing, and teaching in the liberal arts field?

Paul: "I think what a person is is more important than what he knows how to do.

"An educated person should have a wide knowledge of science, language, literature, the arts, psychology, philosophy, history, economics, and sociology, plus theology. Education should give a person breadth as well as a narrow range of skills. I'd hate to go though life without some introduction to the different disciplines of human learning as a setting for my job or profession."

Purely and simply, Paul loves literature. He studied the arts because he couldn't help it. He understands his eagerness as God-given. That's justification enough.

Paul: "I was always a reader, and was greatly attracted to the masters as I got acquainted with them. I saw literature as artistry in the beautiful and effective use of words. And also as the expression of great ideas, including the truths of Christianity. I felt one's education must include what's been said, and how it's been said. I majored in college in Latin and Greek, but found more religious content in the English writers than in the classics."

Not to be overlooked is how he inspired others to love literature.

Paul: "I found that reading poems aloud was a pleasure to students and helped them understand. So I used reading to teach poetry. I accumulated a collection of religious poetry, and used selections from this in my preaching and other speaking. I was often asked to entertain groups of people by reading to them. I suppose many will remember me best for these readings.

"I love the poetry of many men and women. But I suppose Robert Browning stands highest for me. He's a great master of words. I like him most for his use of Christian theology and principles. I'll never forget the thrill of discovering him in English III (high school)

61

under Melvin Landis—such poems as 'Saul,' 'An Epistle,' 'Cleon.' "

Paul and Alta kept quickly catching themselves before too hastily judging others. It seemed to be a pact they had made. Living has taught them the absurdity of drawing immovable lines, and the difficulty of trying to defend them.

Paul: "I don't know if I can defend the lines I draw. Of course, I don't know if anyone can—which jokes you're going to laugh at, for instance.

"Anything that's pretty broadly an offense to people I want to work with, I leave those things out. If people won't listen to you because you use a certain kind of language, why use the language?

"There was a time I'd have said I'll never wear anything but a straight-cut coat. Now with all the extra cost and expense, I don't see anything important in it anymore. There was no principle involved in the change. That can be interpreted by people as having no backbone. But there are things I stand for.

"Like social drinking. I think that's something I'd never do. When I was in Europe I simply explained to people that we don't drink it in America, so I can't here. It was so drilled into me as a child I don't think I could change it. I see alcohol as a drug."

Reckless use of money rankles Paul and Alta. Reckless use of time angers them even more. In their judgment, people who are irresponsible with either are truly of the world in the most base and shameful sense.

Paul: "A person who can't get angry doesn't have a very keen moral sense."

Alta: "So it's okay for me to get angry at the sports world! They just do the same thing over and over again. Once I sat and watched the Olympics and they just played the same thing again and again. People just sliding around the same corner. This is spectatoritis to me!

"Little League makes me angry. And I have some big people on my side. It's just an obsession. And it affects the boys' fathers, too. They scold their children if they don't do well enough. And I used to like sports.

"But anything just to look at—like TV. I could get angry with TV, but I just don't bother with it. I don't have time to look at it."

Paul: "This kind of shallowness, purposelessness, meaninglessness disgusts me, too."

Alta: "Another thing that makes me cross—well, it makes me feel bad—is that the rich get richer at the expense of others. I almost get mad when I think of huge corporations. What do they do with all their money? They don't even know how good it is to give it away."

Paul: "I'm bothered when unions push wages up so inflation rises and people on a fixed income can hardly make it. And a man like Richard Nixon who frittered away great opportunities for mere personal ambition—that was an awful thing."

Paul: (to Alta): "Your husband makes you cross sometimes!"

Alta (to Paul): "Well, that gets over in a minute. That's a different thing!"

Paul: "I wouldn't admit it's impossible to live a Christian life. But we have to work at it.

"We daren't give up and say we won't draw any lines, but we don't have to draw lines for twenty years from now. Someone will take care of that then."

Paul: That's one of our tensions. I'm
inclined to splurge a little.
Alta: Well, can we celebrate without
being extravagant?

7. Celebrating

7. Celebrating

Dare people of such tender conscience celebrate and enjoy it? No easy answer here. The two of them agree in principle but tend to disagree in practice. A little careful splurging now and then can't hurt, Paul thinks.

For Alta it's more serious than that. Celebrating should always be somehow tied up with giving to others. She can't tear the two apart. If you do celebrate, make sure it's meaningful, she cautions.

Paul: "Celebrations—that's one of our tensions. I'm inclined to splurge a little."

Alta: "Well, can we celebrate without being extravagant?"

Paul: "Two weeks from now is her eighty-fifth birthday and we've invited some of our old friends from Ohio and we're gonna have a pretty nice meal, I hope. She would not be inclined to do that."

Alta: "I don't have a craze for celebrating. It'd be wrong for me, I guess."

Paul: "We seldom do it. We seldom go out to eat just for the sake of doing it."

Alta: "For my eightieth birthday on a Sunday, I got a card with eight dimes in it, and I thought, oh, that's clever. On Monday I got another and I thought, uh-oh. On Tuesday I got boxes! On Wednesday night at prayer meeting a man had been seated and got up and came back to me and said, 'How much did you get? How much did you get?' I said I didn't know. It was the fellowship I enjoyed more than the money."

Paul: "Actually, she gave a lot of that away."

Alta: "I was so glad to have all that money to give away. It was over a hundred dollars. I kept the cards."

Paul: "It does me good to be remembered."

Alta: "Well, it does me too."

Paul: "I wouldn't want to be embarrassed with a lot of gifts. But I think I do have a kind of hankering for the recognition that people have appreciated me."

Alta: "At Christmas we had quite a crowd here and we had ham."

Make no mistake. The Erbs have created fun and seized their share of joy through the years. But they've mixed it with care and thought. Seldom was anything done with sheer abandon.

Paul: "One of the things we felt we gave our children was travel. And that was one of the ways they developed their love for the church. At one time Delbert was collecting the signatures of church leaders."

Alta: "There was one he said might die before he got his signature!"

Paul: "For Winifred's graduation gift we took her to the New England States. She was interested in literature.

"We gave our children money all along. We won't have much to give them when we die but we helped them with their houses, Delbert's chicken business, and some trips."

Alta: "One good thing about traveling is when people go on the mission field and stay awhile with their children; they bring something back, *and* help over there."

Paul: "Going to Mennonite World Conference—"

Alta: "That's a celebration for *you!*"

Paul: "Going just to see sights is a very worldly thing if you can't tie it up with some human content. When I went all through Africa I was visiting missions, and Orie Miller looked over my travel plans and saw Victoria Falls and asked, 'Why are you going to the falls?' I said, 'To see the falls.' He would never go out of his way to see that, he said.

"My background in history and literature gave me something to travel with. Did you ever hear of the man who visited Napoleon's tomb and asked, 'Who's Napoleon?' But then I suppose the man had some other merits."

It's true the Erbs have found giving the most au-

thentic way of celebrating. The fact surfaced spontaneously often enough in their conversation to be convincing.

Alta: "When we used to have Christmas exchange we bought each other gifts."

Paul: "What we need we give each other as gifts. But as for surprise gifts, we've had very little inclination for that."

Alta: "I love to give gifts. I like to shop a little bit once in a while."

Paul: "But we're still constantly giving to our children. We bought our children travelers checks when they went to Japan."

Alta: "I believe in helping your children when they need it."

Paul: "Debts worry us."

Alta: "There's Mennonite Broadcasts. I love to give to them."

Paul: "We give to very few causes outside our own church."

Alta: "Last year at Christmas our immediate family decided among ourselves to give money to build houses in Bangladesh."

Paul: "Partly to get rid of the embarrassment of what to get each other. Partly to contribute to our grandchildren's sense of giving."

Alta: "Their enthusiasm is as great as ours. Last year we had a little house on the table with a slit on the top. It looked like a Bangladesh house and we put our money in there. Then this year we had a little grain bag to put the money in for Mennonite Central Committee and their relief food program."

Paul: "For our fiftieth wedding anniversary, instead of having people give us gifts, we had a money box for translating the *Alpha and the Omega* [a book Paul wrote] into Spanish. For our sixtieth anniversary we invited people to contribute to the cost of our son recording music to be used in churches in Argentina."

The principles they share. But the details of celebrating, the nitty-gritty of giving and receiving are still differences between them. Yet they know how to live with that and like it.

Paul: "She is a little bit tight. But not in the sense that she's hoarding. She loves to give just as I do.

"Before Christmas [two months earlier] I picked up a bag of candy, but she put it away where I can't find it!"

Alta: "Two weeks from yesterday we'll put that candy out, okay?"

Change is a good thing and ought to be engineered. We shouldn't make all our changes by default. —Paul.

8. Change

8. Change

Eighty-plus-year-olds can be relaxed about change. Paul and Alta Erb are. It isn't because they are ignorant of it. Nor have they given up in despair.

They just figure change happens, it isn't necessarily bad, it isn't their problem, and worrying about it will do no good.

On this subject they display some of their strongest faith in God and the always emerging church. And they show a special wisdom when they describe what they see. "Change is a good thing and ought to be engineered. We shouldn't make all our changes by default," Paul asserts.

They are relaxed, you see, but they haven't given up the fight.

Paul: "We've lived long enough to see things go in cycles. When I first came into the church, it was anti-necktie. I took mine off, but then I wore it again one Sunday. But I felt so bad I went home, behind the barn on the manure pile, and tore it to shreds so I wouldn't be tempted to wear it anymore!"

Alta: "And now here you wear one."

Paul: "Well, I didn't wear one again until 1960 when I was sixty-six and went to Argentina. My son had said he hoped I wouldn't wear a plain coat because of being confused with Catholics. Then when I went to Eastern Mennonite College in the early seventies an Amish boy asked me why I wore a necktie. Now here's a complete cycle. I wear one and my grandsons don't, for a different reason.

"This shows how old I am but I remember once saying, 'I don't see how any Christian can spend more than $10,000 on a house.' Well, that would be a difficult rule to follow today."

Paul and Alta have the ability to size themselves up with perspective and good humor.

They have found their own footing within the church.

Paul: "When does something need to be changed and when should someone plunge in and change it?

"The fellowship and confidence of the church has always been tremendously important to me. Making a concession for the church has been a common attitude of my life."

Alta: "Did you ever tell Phyllis how you couldn't change on the charismatics?"

Alta's question strikes at the heart of a matter they both feel may threaten the unity of the church. It is one change they find personally painful.

Paul: "I didn't think I'd ever have to meet that issue in the Mennonite Church. I had such a traumatic experience as a boy when my father's church was almost torn apart. I have a deep prejudice against the charismatic viewpoint. I have a deep suspicion about its long-term effects on the church—"

Alta: "And the individuals we've known—"

Paul: "I have something of a reputation, I suppose, as an opponent of the charismatic movement. But I don't want to campaign. I have some fears on this. Am I opposing something some people really need? If they've found something real that I could never bring them with my preaching, then I'd better step back out of the way. If they're right, if there's something here that's good for

the church long-term, then I have confidence that the church will be able to sift it out."

Alta: "Did you hear how he took the floor at Assembly [in Eureka, Illinois, 1975]?"

Paul: "Yes, here I guess I did a little campaigning. I thought people were implying the Holy Spirit's work was new. I used the expression, 'The Holy Spirit's been around for a long time.' And Newton Gingrich, moderator of the Assembly, said, 'Paul Erb's been around for a long time, too!'"

Alta: "And they applauded. Well, he's had experience; he's lived long!"

Paul: "It's the polarization—those who have it and those who don't—that bothers me about the charismatic movement. People go off the deep end emotionally."

No doubt about it, Paul and Alta Erb are more than observers of the change around them. Certain trends trouble them and they say so. But the wisdom they wear keeps them from instinctively labeling "bad" whatever is new or different to them.

Paul: "In the present plethora of change I have some deep concerns. But I'm not addicted to the status quo. For instance, I've discovered they don't have foot washing in some of our churches anymore. And some places it's just a weeknight thing. But I'm not going to let that keep me from dying a happy old man!

"Another disappointment I've had is in MYF [Mennonite Youth Fellowship]. I wanted to integrate the young people with the rest of us. Too much it's become a divisive thing."

Alta: "But I believe a lot of that's been the fault of the older people."

Paul: "Yes, poor sponsorship; the young people are setting themselves off by themselves."

Alta: "Yes, even the youngsters have children's church. We need the intergenerational thing."

Paul: "We're pleading not to break the church up into segments."

Alta: "At EMC each student was assigned an older person and they fellowshiped together and enjoyed it so much. That did me good and I think it did my student some good. I'm collecting illustrations of intergenerational activities."

Paul: "I sounded a little bit negative a while ago about young people, but I've really been well accepted by many of them. I never had worse stage fright than when I stood before my first class at EMC, after being out of the classroom for twenty-five years. At the end of my term at EMC, Myron Augsburger [President of the College,] asked me to speak in chapel. The students gave me a rousing ovation . . . so there's not a generation gap in our church. I'm very happy about our young people.

"I'm not worried about change. It's the Lord's church and that's the spirit with which we go into our old age."

Not worried, but troubled now and then.

Paul: "I gave lectures in my classrooms against attending the theater, but I came to the place where I can see theater as a legitimate form of communication. I figured if you can't beat 'em, join 'em—to many people's great surprise!

"When one of my students saw me in *Hazel's People* [a 35 mm. feature film, set in the Mennonite world, in which Paul has a nonspeaking part as the

grandfather], she wrote to me, 'Now Lord, lettest thy servant depart in peace, for mine eyes have seen Paul Erb in the movies!'

"For a while at Hesston College I opposed the use of all movies, no matter for what. I found the easiest solution to rule them all out. Of course the church then thought that, too. I didn't know where to draw the line.

Even yet, I have a deep innate prejudice against them.

"Looking back I can see time and energy I put into things that have been discarded. I wrote a speech at Hesston against the theater. It was revised several times. Then a few years ago I had a whole bunch left so I threw them away. I thought no one would want to read them anymore.

"I have a little trouble accepting this rock music."

Alta: "Yes, that's been disappointing to me."

Paul: "Once at Vespers at EMC they were singing with guitars without books, songs which I didn't know. I told them I was afraid they'd forget how to sing hymns. And one girl said, 'Let's show him!' So all the rest of the meeting they sang hymns!

"It seems to me that this rock stuff just doesn't say anything. It's so shallow. Let's have a little of this but if we can't keep our hymnody, it's a great disappointment to me."

Their hope prevails. Yet it is more than hope. It is belief.

Paul: "I guess it's chiefly a matter of my confidence in the people who decide. I know we're in another day and this just has to be done."

Sometimes, the way things were done in the past was actually wrong. They are ready to acknowledge that— and their part in it.

Alta: "Lots of people complain about the way we did our mission work, and how it was unwise to make the people we served so dependent on us. But our people, after they leave, are often called back to help. So we shouldn't be too hard on the early missionaries."

Paul: "Well, we shouldn't be hard on them at all. They were living in that colonization time."

Alta: "One great joy I had after we retired was working on Sunday school and vacation Bible school material for children. It took me all over the church. I wrote some of it with Winifred and that was a great pleasure.

"I made adaptations in my writing as I made new discoveries about early childhood."

76

Adaptation, it seems, has been the earmark of their lives.

Paul: "Once in a while when I see that young people have a conscience on things that their parents don't, I think, we'll just have to trust. There will always be young people who can make good, honest judgments. I just have confidence that God's Spirit working in His people is going to find acceptance for good. I don't have to take the attitude that when I'm no longer here things are going to go to pot."

That is the voice of a happy old man!

I formulated a prayer, "God, purge all my motives,"
and I think that's how I forgot what I was doing
that might have been great. —Alta.

9. On Being Significant

9. On Being Significant

Paul and Alta have held leadership positions in the church for decades. One wonders if they have aspired to positions? Do they cherish their power? Is it a pleasure to be significant? Might they have stuck by the church so tightly because they were afraid they couldn't survive in the larger world, or at least be as influential in that bigger pond?

Summing up one's life and assessing one's significance is plainly dangerous. It can also be threatening. The meaning of one's life is a private and precious subject. But Paul and Alta didn't flinch. They answered in humility some very hard questions.

Alta: "One Depression year at Hesston I didn't get anything for teaching. I taught for free."

Paul: "It was glad sacrifice. We believed in church education. We never knew at the beginning of a year what we were going to get. Then after registration my father, who was business manager of the school, sat down and figured what they could pay us. It would have been improper to ask what we were going to get paid. It would have disqualified a person."

Alta: "It was good nurture for us then."

Paul: "I'm not saying that's the way it should be now. This isn't a big nostalgic thing with us, wishing for the good old days."

Their professions had a modest beginning—not the way to start if making a mark were their aim. They had another motivation.

But the taste of prestige was sweet, even so. Yet it didn't overwhelm them. And that's the difference.

Paul: "I think I've been criticized for being ambitious for power and position—and I've had some responsibility. Some people have said I enjoy it too much. I have taken a good deal of satisfaction in some of the positions I've held . . . dean, editor."

Alta: "But you didn't enjoy the prestige."

Paul: "Well, I was tempted."

Alta: "Well, I'm sure you never gloried in it or I'd have caught it."

Paul: "I did try to help other people get a voice."

Alta: "If you'd have been vain I'd have found it out."

Paul: "I did pass up a chance from the University of

Kansas. They offered me a position on the faculty. I think possibly I could have succeeded as a university prof. But it was no temptation at all. I guess I had fears it would take me out of the church."

Alta: "Well, I don't think it was that so much as we felt it wouldn't have been fair to the church. We felt needed."

Paul: "The sacrifice of spiritual ideals would have been very poor. I guess loyalty to the church was dominant. As I've said before, we give very little money except to the Mennonite Church."

Alta: "If more of our church people would give through the church we could really expand our program.

"I had joy in life. I loved to teach. I believe God has used me."

Paul: "She's a born teacher. It's instinct."

Alta: "Well, we all have gifts. I lived as I could and as it worked out.

"The thing maybe that kept me going was that I had a message—like all those men in Saskatchewan and that Sunday school course. I had something to defend and I had something I wanted to get across."

Paul: "Many, many years ago when I was still quite a young man, I was preaching in Kansas City and a young lady slipped in. She leaned forward and stared and stared at me. Afterwards she came to me and said she had a dream about who the next president of the United States would be, and 'You are the man!'" (big laugh).

The idea apparently never went to his head!

Paul: "I was never the person at the top. I was never president of a college or moderator of a conference. I was sort of the chore boy; the tasks were assigned to me."

Alta: "You weren't an A-1 administrator. You were primarily a teacher."

Paul: "Yes, a teacher and preacher."

Alta: "His confidence in God and church made him willing to let the church direct his life and let it interpret his gifts."

It is a peculiar gift—to sense one's own measure and limitations—and accept them freely.

Paul: "I attended the General Conference [of the Mennonite Church] in 1923 in Eureka, Illinois, with my older brother Allen. I remember wondering if I'd ever get to sit on committees!

"Maybe I was ambitious, but ambitious in a good sense. I wanted to make a contribution to the church, and was glad when I could."

Alta: "I think he was a better teacher than dean."

Paul: "There was a reaction against my being too authoritative, too dictatorial when I was dean and in charge of discipline.

"Well, as I mentioned, I was seldom the president of anything. I was often the secretary. I wasn't in the top positions because I wasn't happiest in them.

"I *could* take up dangerous, unhappy situations and give effective, aggressive leadership."

Alta: "Administration wasn't your strong point."

Paul: "Neither am I a first-rate scholar. I'm not a Harold Bender, even though I've done some scholarly things."

One senses a past struggle in the man. Being top dog had its lure. But his sense of service won (with a little help from his prudent wife!).

Paul: "Preaching has been really important to me. I wouldn't say I'm a great preacher, but as things go in the Mennonite Church, I've been something of a trailblazer. I preached some different types of sermons.

"I'm not a pastor but a platform preacher. A young man in VS in Edmonton, Alberta, was struggling with a decision to go to seminary. He wanted to know what I would say. I wrote him that of all the things I've done in my life, for sheer glory to God, and for pleasure—even above my teaching English—preaching was most satisfying.

"I'm a convicted Christian, and so when I'm in the pulpit I'm saying the things I think are the most important for people to think about.

"Times that I have influenced any persons or movements by my preaching, I consider that a success. I rejoice that I can say something people can remember through the years—not for my sake, but because it gave them a guiding light. Directing young people to a philosophy of life—that's where I think I was primarily successful."

He admits to having gotten carried away a few times.

Paul: "At the General Conference in Goshen in 1959, I was Executive Secretary and I also preached the conference sermon—so my church gave me opportunity. That's a big word for me. That night the auditorium was packed to the doors. I had excellent attention. Actually, I don't think I preached a very good sermon. I tried too hard!"

Alta's greatest feeling of achievement came through the church, too. But the church also demanded her biggest sacrifice.

Alta: "The hardest thing I did too was to give up teaching [when the family moved to the Mennonite Publishing House in Scottdale, Pennsylvania, where Paul worked as editor of *Gospel Herald*]. One time we were asked for testimonies in Goshen and I said I was giving up teaching, and not with the same privileges Paul had.

"But at the Publishing House they asked me to teach college courses for which students got credit at Goshen. And I was the librarian.

"And I did get the biggest curriculum job I ever had—working for seven years with a committee, then writing the primary curriculum [published for use in Mennonite Sunday schools], and introducing the materials to the church. That was a great challenge to me."

Paul: "That was a dramatic experience!"

Alta: "In those seven years, I felt all along that my background in teaching gave me something to say, and my colleagues accepted it.

"I formulated a prayer, 'God, purge all my motives,' and I think that's how I forgot what I was doing that might have been great."

The prayer, by all accounts, worked its desired effect.

We have to be severe in judgment on ourselves and withhold judgment of others. —Paul.

10. Answering the Critics

10. Answering the Critics

Public people draw criticism. The question is how seriously those public figures should take their critics.

On the one hand, the critics may be right. A leader must remain sensitive to what the people say. That takes a special grace.

Then too, one may need to act in spite of critics. That also takes special wisdom.

It is still a battle for Paul and Alta.

Alta: "I used to be able to tell when he came over for lunch if he'd gotten a critical letter [as editor of *Gospel Herald*]."

Paul: "I never wanted to be insensitive to criticism. I think I developed sort of an intuitive sense about what would be acceptable. I didn't dismiss criticism. I would ask myself, Why did they say what they said?

"Daniel Kauffman [the previous editor] never used pictures in the *Gospel Herald.* So when I took it over, I had to begin using photos very carefully, very gradually. And I didn't dare use picutres of women without coverings or men without plain coats.

"One of the first pictures I ever printed of a man without a plain coat was of my son Delbert when he was going to South America. One lady wrote in and said he looked more like a gambler than a missionary!

"I just stuck my foot in a little at a time, testing the water.

"I do feel sorry that people made so much of such little things. I don't think I ever developed any hates."

A snapshot of Paul sitting fully-clothed and grinning on a lifeguard's chair on a beach brought other sharp memories to the surface. Paul first explained the picture, and then the agenda behind it.

Paul: "I was at the Allegheny MYF Convention in Camp Rehoboth, Delaware, in 1973. I was out walking on the beach and the lifeguard chair was empty, so I climbed up on it. So it's a falsified picture of a lifeguard!

"Mixed bathing used to be a no-no. In 1926 I went to Oregon to do some soliciting for Hesston College. I drove and took some students from Oregon along. One day they went surf bathing and they said they wished I would join them. So I rented a suit and went in. Some Pacific Coast people reported me back East as an example of the terrible things that were happening.

"This got back to my congregation in Kansas and I had to make a public confession and promise never to do it again. And I kept that promise.

"I tried to adapt in my lifestyle to what the traffic would bear—not grudgingly, but willingly."

Perhaps they could have done better, they believe, by having been more accessible. But there is always one's own personality to be true to.

Paul: "We've both had evidence again and again that people were afraid of us. We've been free to criticize. We've held people off from us. I wish we could have been more friendly."

Alta: "But I wouldn't want to be a dashy-splashy person."

Paul: "So you see, maybe we've gone to the other extreme."

Alta: "I wasn't emotional."

The questions can still torture. But critique should never destroy. These two are sensitive survivors.

How long should I keep going? I guess
as long as they ask me. —Paul

11. Getting Old

11. Getting Old

Is old age peak or valley? Paul and Alta aren't sure. The reality of being old is too close to be quite philosophical about it.

They still have some plans. They haven't dropped out. But sometimes they wonder if they should. Will they have enough wisdom to live this part of life?

Fears exist, to be sure. But active projects, good memories, and hope sustain the Erbs.

Paul: "It's the harvesttime of life. I enjoyed the rough and tumble when I went through the heat of the day, but this is fulfillment. Old age isn't going down hill for us."

Alta: "I'm not enjoying this as much. But it has new features."

Paul: "When we had our young family at home—singing together, the trips we took—it was a very precious time."

Alta: "Yes, it helped me so with my teaching. The students would come around and offer to listen for Winifred crying if I had to go to a meeting at the college."

Paul: "I remember what a delight it was to turn and look at Delbert at the table and he'd always smile! He sat to my right in his high chair.

"Once Winifred had a temper tantrum against her mother and she sat with me and said, 'Father, what makes me like I am?' and I said, 'Well, I guess it's because I'm you father and I have a temper!' "

Alta: "Once Winifred said when they had a shower for someone and they brought so many presents, 'Why don't you and Father get married again so we can have a shower and have nice presents.' "

As alive as their memories, are their old passions.

Alta: "I had the privilege of selecting books for libraries or missionary families when someone gave them fifty or seventy-five dollars to spend for books. What I think has been a great service—"

Paul: "You began that after we went to Goshen—"

Alta: "—the Gospel Bookstore would give me books to take out to churches for family conferences to sell. And I did it at Family Week at Laurelville. People wanted to buy books for their children."

Paul: "And they trusted her recommendation. And she sold them without a commission."

Alta: "This was a great privilege. I had to ask if people would be interested in children's books.

"I hope this will be carried on. I also carried parents' books. It's very necessary. I still try to interest children and their parents in good literature by reviewing many books for *Provident Bookfinder*.

"In my retirement years I've kept up particularly in reading about preschool children. I read much in preschool education. God has certainly prepared the

child for learning: physically, intellectually, socially, and spiritually. Parenthood has been exalted to new heights as we've learned how important the spiritual environment of the home is."

Paul: "The major objectives of my life have been accomplished. I've done enough in different areas to keep me satisfied. But the Lord keeps giving me opportunties. I thought that my productive life was finished before I went to EMC in 1969, at the age of 75.

"I'd like to do some writing yet. Somebody told me there ought to be a simpler version of *The Alpha and the Omega*. So I wrote a popularized paperback version of my prophetic viewpoints.

"I titled the new book *Bible Prophecy: Questions and Answers*. The publisher encouraged me in this, and approved my idea for a question and answer format. The style is simpler than the earlier book and the paperback binding kept the cost down. Alta helped me write by listening to an oral reading of each unit as I finished writing, and giving me her reactions. She's an excellent critic.

"And I heard a suggestion that there ought to be a collection of Mennonite humor. I considered doing that for a while."

Alta: "I like my opportunities in helping people teach preschool children. I'd like the opportunity to help parents through writing or speaking."

Alta's enthusiasm for cultivating young minds is undimmed. It's notorious. Her grasp of how to teach is perhaps her greatest gift.

Alta: "Long ago I discovered that teaching and learning are two different activities. I couldn't 'learn' my

students. They had to do that themselves. So what was my job? I had to plan what they would have to do in order to learn. Teaching became my arranging for their learning to take place. To this day, that is my best approach to teaching any subject matter. Often I had to prepare some special approach for a special pupil. Not all students liked math. So I had to ponder how one learns that if $3x - 10 = 20$, then $x = 10$. I couldn't always remember how I had learned it.

"When I taught elementary education I again had to study how children learn—in spelling, history, geography, language, and all the subjects."

Paul: "Her book, *The Christian Nurture of Children,* written in 1944, on Christian education is still appreciated by students although it recently went out of print."

Alta: "I always tried to introduce my students to great books for children—books made by good authors and good artists. As a child I didn't read many books because they weren't available. We had no libraries in our elementary schools. Some of my students, especially older women preparing to return to teaching, had read few if any children's books. Here was a new subject to study. We tried to become like little children, and went together on many happy journeys through books."

A few regrets linger. Some questions gnaw.

Paul: "I think a Christian is one who wins others to Christ and I haven't done a lot of that. I haven't known how to do this. I'd rather read a book than talk to the person beside me. Oh, I did some of it. I may have helped a hitchhiker a little once."

Alta: "One thing I think about with regret is that I

could read and sing without thinking. I was so good at memorizing and that got me by. I got an A in philosophy without knowing anything about philosophy."

Paul: "How long should I keep going? I guess as long as they keep asking me."

Alta: "Well, because of the kind of work we were in, there's more carry-over than for someone who's worked in a garage and suddenly has to stop."

Paul: "Everything now in my life is a bonus."

Alta: "Going to Vermont was a gift."

Paul: "It's something of a problem for me whether I should accept invitations. I believe in the principle of retirement; the old should get out of the way. And maybe I should turn down invitations and just say, 'I'm too old.' I fear they'll ask me to speak because they think I want to, when I shouldn't."

Alta: "Oh, your family'll tell you if you shouldn't. We have the kindness of Winifred and Milford opening up their home."

Paul: "Well, we have hundreds of friends who tell us they appreciate us and we know they mean it."

The unknowns are as foreboding at this time of life as at any other. But then the comforts and securities may be greater—at least for the fortunate.

Alta: "Winifred invited us to come and live with them when their children were all gone. [Paul and Alta moved there in June 1973.] Our granddaughter Alta is a good licensed practical nurse and she says she'll care for us when we get incapacitated.

"Our church's old people's homes don't seem to be for us."

Paul: "We live very much together. Alta and I have

two rooms we call our own—our living room/sitting room/sewing room, and a bedroom with closets. Then their living room and kitchen are ours, too.

"They get up and leave in the morning—they both work—before we're up, and get home for supper by 5:30 or 5:45.

"Some families would have problems, but we haven't. We don't pay them so much a month. Whoever goes to the store pays for the groceries. And when some of the bills come—I get the mail in the morning—I just pay them."

Alta: "I don't believe I have any fears."

Paul: "Of course, we're hoping we don't have a long invalidism. But if it comes, I guess we'd try to make that a rich experience.

"If I'd become senile and didn't realize it—"

Alta: "Maybe we are."

Paul: "—that, I hope we'd be spared.

"This thing of driving. It's hard for any man to give up driving."

Alta: "Well, last year for a birthday greeting, Winifred and Milford promised to take you on any long trips, and even anywhere around home. They are very kind."

Paul: "I hadn't had any accident, and my license to drive was still good. Winifred simply reasoned that a person in his eighties has lost some of his sharpness, and I couldn't argue against that. It was not only that I feared being injured in an accident. I didn't want to carry the regret of having injured or killed someone else.

"I think I have a constructive attitude toward old age.

One of my favorite bits of poetry is, 'Grow old along with me. . . .'

"It's different than any other stage of life."

Alta: "But you come into it gradually."

Paul: "A ripe fruit is different from any other of its stages."

Growth continues even in these years. And struggle persists.

Buoyed by the feeling they are still needed, their reservoir of memories, and lively hope, Paul and Alta confess that these years are mostly rich. They understand it could be otherwise.

Wisely they have permitted their past and their future to invade and color their present years. And so they have not faded; neither have they escaped life. Their days are full.

Paul: "Just the memories. . . . I think there's probably seldom a day that in my reading I don't see mentioned a place where I have been. This is a great joy—those images. I have a big treasure house of them."

Alta: "The best thing I have now is intercession—my prayer book."

Paul: "She's constantly revising her book."

Alta: "Well, it gets too full. I just put in all new pages on Brazil. Oh, it's so full! I try especially to keep up on the single women."

Paul: "There's a new *Mennonite Yearbook* just coming off the press and she wants me to get her one of her own that she can cut up for her prayer book."

Alta: "Yes, I'm a prayer partner. I get lots of letters from these people."

Paul and Alta Erb are some of the oldest apprentices

you may find. They update constantly but never fad-dishly. They adapt, they prepare, they practice.

At Assembly '75 in Eureka, Illinois [a gathering of several thousand North American Mennonites], Paul joined the Assembly Choir. It was summer and it was stifling in the Auditorium where the choir stood squeezed together sweating as they sang. Paul stood near the back of the group, next to one of his old Scott-dale cronies, Joe Buzzard.

First the choir taught the audience some new songs. Then they belted out the "Hallelujah Chorus." Af-terward Paul explained with a hearty laugh why he chose to be a member of this group which sang at nearly every session.

"I've been telling people, facetiously, that the reason I'm helping to sing is because I expect to be up 'There' [pointing in the direction of the sky] pretty soon, and I don't want Gabriel to bawl me out for not observing a rest!"

A mix of responsibility and relaxation characterize Paul and Alta's living these days. It is a wonderful min-gling.

Their biggest jobs are over and the results can't be changed. They know that. But they aren't quitters either. They'll be earning their board, and doing what needs to be done when asked, until they're invited into the next world.

Paul: "As an older person I've taken the position that I won't offer my advice, and I won't go around as a cam-paigner on subjects—unless people ask me. I want to die happy. I want to die with a minimum of concerns, so things I don't need to worry about, I won't worry about."

I'm not worried about change. It's the Lord's church and that's the spirit with which we go into our old age. —Paul.

Paulisms and Altaisms

Paulisms and Altaisms

Paul and Alta are masters of the quotable quote. Their choicest lines are never canned. They simply roll out, spontaneously.

Listed here by subject, clearly to the point despite being pulled out of context, are Paulisms and Altaisms I prize.

On Marriage

"Married people need to compromise but you can't take turns compromising. You shouldn't keep those kinds of books in married life."—Alta.

"Continue to become the kind of person your mate can admire."—Paul.

"One thing that keeps me from being a male chauvinist is observing that God just didn't make women to be submerged."—Paul.

"We ought to have our whole personalities married but it oughtn't be static. You can have some things in tension."—Paul.

"It's a nice theory that you get lost in each other, but it just isn't practical, is it? Each individual just keeps developing."—Alta.

"This talk that a husband and wife must find out which is the boss—that makes no sense to us."—Paul.

On Children

"You can adapt to any living situation (within limits) and be happy, if you're willing to make children more important than your house."—Alta.

"I think children must know their father's vocation. A caring father keeps his children close."—Alta.

"There ought to be, in this day of the automobile, more family traveling projects."—Paul.

"We must make our homes so attractive that the children won't want to go everywhere else."—Alta.

"Work with what you have. If you can't have family worship every evening, have it once a week."—Paul.

On Possessions and Things
"It's difficult to be totally simple. You can magnify the symbol of simplicity above the reality of it."—Paul.

"We ought to preach simplicity but not legislate it." —Paul.

"A man who gets into business and is successful is in an awful dangerous spot."—Paul.

"Now that young man we know who became a millionaire—he has a problem."—Alta.

"I don't think if you live simply you're necessarily Christian, but if you are a Christian I think you'll live simply."—Alta.

"I don't believe we lived simply to earn any merit from God."—Alta.

"I pity anyone who grows up in an abundant economy where they can get anything they want."—Paul.

On Being Separate
"I want to be where the brave minority is."—Paul.

"There's no one way of living. We have had fellowship with people whose way of living we didn't have to copy."—Atla.

"I'd say I'm nonconformed in setting a table; I wouldn't have felt right to take the time or the money to serve a fancy meal on expensive dishes."—Alta.

"I wouldn't admit it's impossible to live a Christian life. But we have to work at it."—Paul.

On Drawing Lines
"I don't know if I can defend the lines I draw. Of course, I don't know if anyone can."—Paul.

"A person who can't get angry doesn't have a very keen moral sense."—Paul.

"We don't have to draw lines for twenty years from now. Someone else will take care of that then."—Paul.

"You live your way without criticizing other people in front of your children."—Alta.

"We ought to get the attitude and the idea first, and then get the word."—Alta.

"You can't draw lines for other people but you're lost if you don't for yourself."—Paul.

On Celebrating
"Can we celebrate without being extravagant?" —Alta.

On Change
"I made adaptations. . . ."—Alta

"Change is a good thing and ought to be engineered. We shouldn't make all our changes by default."—Paul.

"I've now accepted some changes I once would have been alarmed about."—Paul.

"The actual change made sometimes is not as important as the process by which it happens—if it's by defiance, or deciding as a group."—Paul.

On Being Significant
"It wouldn't be good for my soul to prepare a meal for people to talk about."—Alta

"I don't have to take the attitude that when I'm no longer here things are going to go to pot."—Paul.

Answering the Critics

"I tried to adapt in my lifestyle to what the traffic would bear—not grudgingly, but willingly."—Paul.

"I wouldn't be so afraid of criticism anymore in bringing up children."—Alta.

"We can't insist on our solution being taken by others."—Paul.

Getting Old

"I believe in the principle of retirement; the old should get out of the way."—Paul.

"I want to keep up to date."—Alta.

"As an older person I've taken the position that I won't offer my advice, and I won't go around as a campaigner on subjects—unless people ask me."—Paul.

"I'm just doing some of my learning now."—Alta.

"I'm not worried about change. It's the Lord's church and that's the spirit with which we go into our old age."—Paul.

Father often repeated, "Be not the last to lay the old aside, nor yet the first by whom the new is tried."
—Winifred (Erb) Paul

Letters About Paul and Alta

Letters About Paul and Alta

I include Alta and Paul Erb in my collection of "People I'd Like to Keep" (the title of a book by Mary O'Neill). They are among the very favorites on my roster of the humble great I've been privileged to know.

Their ability to keep a delicate balance between genuine humility and an honest awareness of their God-given gifts has freed them to be confident and assured as they exercise those gifts.

Ada Schrock
Salisbury, Pennsylvania

During the 1940s when I was in charge of the mission station at Locust Grove, near Elkhart, Indiana, we rented Paul and Alta's car to haul teachers the twelve-mile trip from Goshen to the little Locust Grove Church. They were always very willing to let us use their Ford V8. Of course, we paid them a small amount for each trip, but I'm sure it didn't cover the actual expenses. It was the only automobile they had. They made many sacrifices in being without a car during those years that we used it. This has been their attitude all the way along, not only with their automobile but with everything they had.

Russell Krabill
Elkhart, Indiana

Alta made her religious commitment early in life. This commitment obviously denied her nothing of pleasure but rather increased the depth and abundance of her nature—initiative, energy, intellectual inquiry, and practical common sense.

Melva Kauffman
Hesston, Kansas

I shall never forget those severe depression years in 1934 and 1935 when the Paul Erbs lived on a $35 a month wage, just so Hesston College could keep its program going.

Mabel Erb Kauffman
Hesston, Kansas

The word that comes to my mind first is integrity. Paul is a church statesman. In writing the *Alpha and Omega*, prophecy was an issue that was ripping the church apart and he saw that. The publication of the book bridged that gap and set that issue to rest in the Mennonite Church.

Yes, Paul had the ability to bring divergent groups together. Statesmanship may imply compromise, but he clearly was a person of integrity.

Carl Kreider
Goshen, Indiana

It happened frequently on chorus tours that the host congregation would serve a meal for the chorus before an evening program. Paul would usually caution the chorus members to "go easy on the pie." Pie was *bad* for singers. Then would come the reminder, "But I'm the director; I don't need to sing."

Earnest Kauffman
West Point, Nebraska

During the years when our sons were young we often attended the annual Mission Board Meetings. Our boys spent much time around the book display where Alta was usually employed. Sometimes she permitted Ron to help pack and unpack books. The Erbs always made our sons feel "special." Paul even asked Ron to eat with him a few times. They made children feel a part of the church.

Marjorie Yoder Guengerich (Mrs. Paul T.)
Harrisonburg, Virginia

Mrs. Buzzard had shown me how to make braided rugs and I had one in the making. When I showed it to Mrs. Erb she told me I shouldn't waste my time making rugs. (I am about to tell you something pleasing about her.) I kept this saying in my heart, not as much as a reprimand as a puzzlement. Why shouldn't I make a rug!

Imagine my surprise and pleasure in paying her a visit twenty-five years later to find her sitting in the midst of a rug production project, not making one measly rug as I had done but dozens of them—and with her usual excitement and dedication.

Mrs. Erb is a woman who sets priorities and follows through on them. The years have a way of leveling out one's interests. It permits her to braid rugs.

J.D. Graber
Goshen, Indiana

I can remember when Paul turned fifty. I was very upset and sad thinking that he was getting so old, and that he might soon become inactive. How wrong I was! Now I'm that age and he is still going strong at 80 plus. He seems to me now to be the same age I thought him to be at fifty.

Mrs. David Derstine
Blooming Glen, Pennsylvania

Both Paul and Alta used their professional skills effectively in their Christian calling. They remained intellectually alert and open to new ideas and changing situations.

Paul Bender
Goshen, Indiana

Anyone who is charitable, who seeks all the evidence and weighs it, as each of them has done, can't be harsh about the past or cynical about the future.

Their simple but firm Christian faith—all the principles and ethics—are very real to Paul and Alta.

A. J. Metzler
Elkhart, Indiana

The Erbs have given me an example of loyalty to the church. I know few persons who are as staunchly loyal—not in an unstudied manner but in a careful questioning way. I have learned important things about loyalty from them.

I think a strength for both of them is that they have worked together on so many things. When they went

out on family conferences they presented the husband-wife dialogue that made for a well-rounded presentation.

Helen Alderfer
Scottdale, Pennsylvania

As a small boy, I was given educational toys, although these were often homemade, or else I spent hours looking at books that mother used in her classes. Interest in geography came from their ample collection of road maps. I spent many hours sitting in the car imagining that I was driving on the roads that I followed on the map. When I was older and could really drive, I already knew many of the roads in the Midwest by heart.

Our church in Kansas where I accepted Christ and was baptized was quite conservative in its time. Some members of our congregation considered the radio as something of the devil. So as long as we lived in Kansas we never had a radio, not because my parents considered it a sin, but rather because they respected those to whom they were to minister as pastors. Nor did I wear a necktie until we moved to Indiana. However, once we made the move, there was no questioning—we got a radio and my folks bought me a tie.

My father always respected the regulations of the church, especially when it involved his ministry as is the case with the plain coat. However, my parents were not legalistic and when the time for change came they accepted it as the natural thing. This has helped me to interact with those who are legalistic. It has also helped me to understand that the principle behind a regulation is the important thing and that I need not get upset when customs and regulations change.

Some would probably say that my dad was away from home too much. But my parents' interest in the church and their dedication to the cause of the church became a part of me. I soon discovered that few young people my age enjoyed attending church business meetings or conferences.

Many children start collections. Among several that I had was collecting the signatures of church leaders. I started this at my father's suggestion since he thought it might be more interesting and valuable than milk bottle caps or railroad freight car numbers.

Mother was both teacher and homemaker. Cooking was usually simple. When we invited students to the house or visitors arrived unannounced there was little difficulty, because our family never expected that anything fancy or expensive had to be made. With hungry students around the table most of the food usually disappeared. In this case my dad's standard joke was, "Well, it looks like my wife made just enough." It was just a part of the practical way my mother did things. She never liked to have leftovers.

J. Delbert Erb
Buenos Aires, Argentina

say that he invested energy in the 1940s on some things that probably wouldn't worry him today. His sense of humor saved us both as we discussed a hat I wore. Most Goshen College girls did without hats. Mine was not only brilliant red, it even had a feather! Since neither of us could make a case for the hat, the color, *or* the feather, I retired the useless garment from my life. Nor was I offended by the conversation.

Dorothy McCammon
Goshen, Indiana

My faith was in Paul Erb first, and that makes sense. Love, patience, wisdom, compassion, humor, tolerance, courage—these traits incarnate—are convincing. These traits of his, faithfully lived out, became bridges. Professor Erb was my John the Baptist. He showed me, then introduced me to Jesus Christ.

Can I recall a weakness of Paul Erb? I guess I'd just

112

I believe my parents influenced my life more than most parents. I didn't have lots of brothers and sisters to spend time with, so for them to live with us seems very natural to me. Except for two years in the dorms at Hesston and Goshen I've always lived close to my parents.

Another reason they influenced me is that they were my teachers in high school and college, and all my life I saw them in other capacities than my parents. Father was the dean at Hesston, the preacher at our church, the churchman all around the country, the head of the English department when I was in college. Mother was a teacher, superintendent of Summer Bible school and Sunday school. My closest association was in the years when they were teachers. So I do not remember them chiefly for cooking or serving me, but as they served a vast group of Mennonites.

I'm not sure how they influenced me, but I'm sure their many varied interests came through. Father's love for poetry made me love it. Their good taste in music influenced me. Father's love of travel; Mother's interest in little children from a scientific point of view; Father's interests in birds, his hatred of fixing things; Mother's good taste in decorating, sewing, pictures, dressing; Mother's ability to teach; Father's vast knowledge; their love of the church; Mother's simple cooking; Father's sense of direction and his love of people; Mother's interest in people and her great ability to organize—these all must have influenced me.

One reason they were good teachers is because they spent hours in preparation. For Father's lecture on Job at EMC he read ten books. Mother spends hours on a Sunday school lesson, and did the same when she taught college. Her class notes were always down on paper.

Oh yes—they loved to entertain with simple fare. Mother used to have every student at Hesston in our home—during Depression years. They were very good about letting cousins and others live in our house while attending Hesston.

Father often repeated, "Be not the last to lay the old aside, nor yet the first by whom the new is tried," and I think that maxim has governed my life in the church.

Winifred (Erb) Paul
Scottdale, Pennsylvania

Paul and Phyllis

Phyllis Pellman Good first learned to know Paul and Alta Erb when Paul spent summers answering visitors' questions at Dutch Family Festival in Lancaster, Pennsylvania.

The Festival was one of several interpretive projects related to Mennonite and Amish identity undertaken by Phyllis and her husband, Merle. She has written and directed several short plays performed in the Festival Theater, is associate director of The People's Place in Intercourse, Pennsylvania, and is editor of *Festival Quarterly,* a magazine which explores the art, faith, and cultures of Mennonite peoples.

Phyllis Good grew up in Millersville, Pennsylvania. She received her BA and MA in English from New York University and has taught English at Lancaster Mennonite High School. She is active in the Landisville Mennonite Church, and is the mother of a young daughter, Kate.

Paul M. Schrock is a well-known free-lance photographer in the religious field. Thousands of his photographs have appeared during the past decade in the Christian education curricula and the magazines of many publishers.

In addition, he maintains a full schedule as Book Editor for Herald Press, Scottdale, Pennsylvania. He grew up on a rye grass farm near Albany, Oregon. He graduated from Western Mennonite School, received his BA in Secondary Education and English from Eastern Mennonite College, and his MA in Journalism at Syracuse University.

Paul and his wife, June (Bontrager), are active in the Kingview Mennonite Church, Scottdale, Pennsylvania, and are the parents of Carmen, Brent, and Andrea.

Schrock was particularly suited for this photographic assignment because of his long friendship with Paul and Alta Erb and his admiration for them as unique individuals.